DON'T BE
A FINANCIAL
DISASTER

—————— *by* ——————

Scott B. Zuckerman
ChFC®, CFS®, CLU®, ChSNC®

DON'T BE A FINANCIAL DISASTER

ISBN: 978-0-578-82199-3

The opinions voiced in this material are for general information only
and are not intended to provide specific advice or recommendations
for any individual. No content should be construed as legal,
tax, or investment advice. Always consult an attorney, or a tax
or investment professional regarding your specific situation.

This material contains only general descriptions and is not
a solicitation to sell any insurance product or security.

There is no guarantee that a diversified portfolio will enhance
overall returns or outperform a non-diversified portfolio.
Diversification does not protect against market risk.

Please keep in mind that insurance companies alone determine
insurability and some people may be deemed uninsurable because
of health reasons, occupation, and lifestyle choices. Any guarantees
are based on the claims paying ability of the issuing company.

CONTENTS

PREFACE

When I was just thirteen years old, I discovered I had the bug of entrepreneurship running through my veins; Scott's Tennis Racket Stringing and Sales was launched! At sixteen, I became a professional magician, and in college I started a DJ business. Little did I know these teenage endeavors would be the start of my entrepreneurial journey, which would lead to successes, and, of course, failures.

I grew up in an affluent town in Long Island, New York, where my family owned and operated a very successful retail jewelry operation. When I was a child, my father would bring me to his office. My training started with sorting plastic bags, then I learned how to ship packages, solder precious metals, and as I got older, I learned how to sell and manage a staff. I never dreamed of going into the jewelry business (and I didn't), but the experience my father and grandfather afforded me helped shape me into the successful businessman I am today.

While in high school, I took interest in legal studies after attending the "law club" elective. In addition, I played an active role in the competitive mock trial team. I attended Syracuse University and chose a pre-law major, with the intention of attending law school after I graduated. It's interesting how life just happens. Upon graduating college, my desire to attend law school faded, and the entrepreneurial bug bit me again.

When I graduated in 1999, the internet was booming, and it seemed if you had a good idea for a dot-com, you could be rich! I thought there must be a way I could capitalize by starting an online business of my own, and this is when WeLoveToParty.com was launched. My parents were supportive of me and handed over all the money that was gifted to me throughout the years. It came to about $40,000. I decided to invest all of it into my new business venture, and having good credit, I was able to secure a loan for an additional hundred thousand dollars. Without getting into the details of what the company did, I was sure I had figured out a way to revolutionize the entertainment industry with my new dot-com idea.

After being in business for a little over a year and proving to have some success, I approached venture capitalists about investing in the company. While this was a challenge, I did receive some interest. So what happens next, you might be wondering. Well, this story doesn't end too well. When the Nasdaq crashed in 2000 and 2001, banks and venture capital firms froze most of the funding they were providing to dot-coms. To make matters worse, later in 2001 terrorist attacks rocked New York City and our nation. Not only was I not able to secure an investment for my great idea, but most of our clients had cut their entertainment budgets. I was basically out of business, and at this point, I was twenty-four years old and $200,000 in debt. One year later, I had to declare bankruptcy.

Besides my dreams being shattered, I was now broke, had no job, and was trying to support myself, living in one of the most expensive cities in the world. I thought perhaps I should just go into the family business. Oddly enough, my family's business was also having financial troubles, and after fifty years in business, they were about to declare bankruptcy as well.

I felt so defeated and had no clue what I was going to do with my life. I started putting my resume out there to get a "job," but I knew having something of my own was a must! How could I ever work for someone else after being my own boss for the last couple of years? I had made so many mistakes building my first "real" company. These mistakes, coupled with watching a fifty-year-old family business sink like the Titanic, led me to my destiny.

While searching for jobs online, I came across advertisements to enter the financial services industry and learn to do financial planning. Wow! This could not come at a better time. Not only did I need to do some serious planning of my own, but I wanted to learn everything possible to help other businesses and individuals so they never find themselves in a situation like mine or my family's business.

I found a firm that was willing to train me and pay for several years of graduate-level study so I could learn how to become an expert in my new field. I was anxious to start getting clients of my own, so I teamed up with a Certified Financial Planner at the firm. This gave me the ability to experience real-world examples of how powerful proper planning is. I witnessed firsthand how mistakes can absolutely devastate a person or a business, so I dove in headfirst with my colleague, and embarked on my mission to help as many people and businesses as I could.

Seven years into my career I opened my own firm. I have several advisors who work on my team and multiple staff members supporting us and our clients. With now over twelve years in the industry, my mission continues to change people's lives every single day.

WHAT IS FINANCIAL PLANNING, ANYWAY?

Depending on how old you are, you may remember individuals calling themselves stockbrokers or life insurance salesmen. These sales job titles are not used much anymore because many would consider them "dirty" words. Today if you tell someone you're a stockbroker or that you sell life insurance, the conversation probably stops there.

Reputations of these salespeople slowly deteriorated throughout the years because many bad apples spoiled the bunch. It's not to say these professions don't still exist, but now they call themselves something different—a financial advisor, planner, consultant, or whatever other fancy title they decide to use. Don't get me wrong, part of financial planning may be choosing stocks or include purchasing a life insurance policy, but it's the implementation method that is most important. I always say you can train a monkey to sell financial products, but the expertise of building a comprehensive plan for the client's benefit is a unique skill. This takes years of advanced education, experiential learning, advocacy, and relationship building.

Imagine building a house with no foundation. It would be impossible to start framing the walls before the foundation is laid. Like building a house, most things have a process. If we don't follow these specific steps, it's very difficult to obtain a favorable result. When it comes to financial planning, I often call a lack of process as developing a financial junk drawer. This is when you accumulate various financial products throughout your life when you think you need them. Once a year you pull out the statements to do your taxes or pay an invoice, and then the paperwork goes back into the file cabinet. Do you even know why you have those products? When was the last time you checked for rate increases? Have you verified your beneficiaries are still valid and correct? Have you taken advantage of all available tax deductions or made sure your investments are tax efficient? Have you rebalanced your 401(k) or IRA? Do you have an old 401(k) from a company you no longer work for? Have you reviewed your will, living will, health care proxy, and power of attorney? And the list goes on and on.

> *The process of financial planning should be broken down into five main components: cash flow, asset protection, asset accumulation, asset distribution, and asset preservation.*

Cash flow is the foundation of your "financial house." This is the first place you should start when building your plan. This is where you can see what comes in and out of your financial life, the difference between your fixed and discretionary expenses, and what is left over for saving.

Related to cash flow are three very important concepts: velocity of money, lost opportunity cost, and arbitrage. These economic concepts should be considered when examining your cash flow. Velocity of money is the rate in which money changes hands and how it is used. Lost opportunity cost is what you could've done with your money that was used for something completely useless or inefficient.

Think about how banks make their money. They want deposits, and they want the money to stay at the bank for as long as possible. If you borrow money from a bank, it charges you an interest rate. When you pay money back, they again loan it to someone else. The same dollar is being used over and over again for them to continuously make money. As an example, let's assume you want to purchase a car for $5,000. You borrow money from the bank to make the payment. You then go to the car dealership to pay for the car. The car dealership takes that same money and deposits it back into the bank. Then the bank can go and relend that same $5,000. That same $5,000 can be used multiple times to turn a profit. With a clear understanding of how money actually works, you can figure out ways to use your own cash flow in a similar manner.

Lost opportunity cost, or the missed opportunity of what you could be doing instead of something else, can be detrimental to your planning. For example, many people will purchase insurance when they buy a car or home and not look at their insurance policies for years. The insurance companies know this, and they will raise their rates throughout the years. Many people won't even pay attention, especially if they set up their account on autopay. Taking this further, let's assume your initial premium was $1,200 per year. After not checking, it increases to $1,800 per year. Assuming you could reduce that premium with another company but don't, the extra $600 you are paying is a lost opportunity cost. If you invested those extra funds instead of paying too much for your insurance, it could add up to significant dollars over the long term. Now take this same concept and apply it to everything you pay for.

Arbitrage is another important concept to understand. It can be applied to cash flow (as you will see in a moment) and is often used by traders for complex investment strategies. Arbitrage is the exploitation of price differences between different financial markets to make a profit, with a minimal amount of risk.

This example will clarify arbitrage for you: Suppose there were two farmers markets in your city. One of them (Market A) sold a particular type of orange for $2 a pound. Market B sold identical oranges for $3 a pound. You could simply buy oranges at Market A and then stroll over to Market B and sell them. How could you lose?

When examining your cash flow, you should try to identify arbitrage situations. While debt can be considered negative in many situations, many sophisticated and diligent investors can use debt to their advantage. Suppose you are considering a home renovation project, and while you have the cash to complete the project, perhaps it could make sense not to use that cash. With interest rates being so low now, perhaps you can secure a line of credit or personal loan for 3 percent. If you think you can earn more than 3 percent in your investment accounts over time—6 percent, as an example, creating a 3 percent gain—then you would be better off in the end using the loan to create the arbitrage. This could become dangerous if you didn't actually use the money to make an investment and just continued to take on more debt. The point is, arbitrage can be a very useful strategy to pay yourself first so you can continue to build your assets while being smart servicing what could now be considered good debt.

Next, it is important to review all insurance coverages in detail, the **asset protection** component. This includes but is not limited to auto, home, umbrella, life, disability, and long-term care. Each of these should be looked at to ensure sufficient coverage and cost.

Asset accumulation is where you focus on your savings. You want to examine how much cash flow should be directed to short- and long-term liquid savings, emergency fund, college savings (if you have children and want to save for their education), investments in both qualified (retirement) and nonqualified accounts (not retirement), and real estate (not including your primary residence).

How do you know if you will ever run out of money during your retirement? This question should be answered during the **asset distribution** analysis. Surely, we can't rely on Social Security alone to live our golden years. In addition, many Americans rely on jobs that offer pensions. While these pensions certainly help, they still may not be enough. That said, jobs that offer pensions are becoming harder to find. For these reasons among many others, a well-thought-out accumulation strategy is paramount.

What happens when you are no longer here? Do you want to die penniless, or leave a legacy to your family or charity? If you have minor children, what happens if they suddenly became orphaned? Who will care for your children? What happens in the event of your incapacitation and you can't make your own financial or medical decisions? These important questions can be answered within several legal documents and are reviewed during the **asset preservation** conversation. While not the most pleasant topic to discuss during financial planning, it can easily be determined one of the most important. Two things are guaranteed in life— death and taxes. Therefore, the inevitable must be reviewed and carefully planned for.

Okay...so now what? Choosing the right financial professional is very important. Avoid the mistaken belief that all financial professionals are equally skilled and capable. Abilities and ethics vary from one person to another. It's your money, so ensure that you're protecting it and getting the best service possible. Take your time and find someone who fits your personality and needs. Choose someone you can develop a long-lasting relationship with. You want to find an advisor who wants to earn your trust, not one who expects it.

Remember what I said earlier about the difference between a salesperson and a true planner? I always recommend choosing a financial planner who has credentials. For example, Certified Financial Planners and Chartered Financial Consultants have different certifications. Accountants may or may not have a CPA. Find out what credentials your prospective expert has and verify them. Ensure that you understand what each of the credentials means and how their process works.

Understanding every decision you make is important, and if you hire an expert to help you, they should educate you during each component of planning including their process. You should come armed with questions. How will you be charged? A percentage? By the hour? By the job? Determine how the company generates its income. Is this acceptable to you? How does that compare to the competition? Is this person worth the cost? Do they work as part of a team, including other professions like CPAs and attorneys?

In conclusion, spend the necessary time to find the right financial professional for you. Determine your goals and then find the best person to fulfill them. Below you will find a worksheet to help get you started on goal planning. We will spend some more time on goal setting in future chapters.

ORGANIZING THE FINANCIAL JUNK DRAWER WORKSHEET

Cleaning out the garage or junk drawer in your kitchen helps keep your home neat. Don't you think it's time to organize the financial junk drawer too?

By answering the following questions, you can increase your understanding of your financial situation and move forward toward your financial goals.

1. How can I enhance my current filing system for my financial documents?

2. Do I have adequate life insurance? How do I know?

_____

_____

_____

_____

_____

3. Do I have an emergency fund and a plan for saving for it? If not, how can I get started on this process?

_____

_____

_____

_____

4. Do I have a will and an estate plan? If not, what do I need to do to create these? Where can I find a legal expert to help me?

_____

_____

_____

_____

_____

5. Does my cash flow fit my financial situation and support my financial goals? If not, list monthly expenses here to get a quick idea of what may need to change.

_____

_____

_____

_____

_____

_____

_____

_____

6. Do I have disability insurance to pay my expenses if I become unable to work? How much do I need?

_____

_____

_____

_____

_____

_____

_____

7. What is my investment plan? Do my investments have an appropriate amount of risk for my circumstances? Should I increase my diversification? Will I have enough to retire comfortably?

_____

_____

_____

_____

_____

_____

Additional notes:

SIX COSTLY MISTAKES
YOU WANT TO AVOID

I often hear from clients that sometimes it seems like the financial part of their lives is the most challenging area in which to succeed.

Sometimes you may find there's something that moves us backward instead of ahead toward a bright financial future. Maybe it's unexpected medical expenses. Perhaps the car or house needs repair. You might suddenly find yourself between jobs! Life has a strange way of throwing us negative curveballs to deal with.

If you've ever felt there may not be a way out, then you'll be glad to know you are certainly not alone. Good news is on the horizon.

I have spoken with many of my colleagues throughout the years, and we all tend to agree that most people tend to make several major financial mistakes that hold us back.

If you could just avoid those mistakes, think how much easier your life would be! You could sail on the wings of financial freedom instead of feeling like you're wallowing in the mire.

Below you'll discover six common mistakes I often see, and you'll learn helpful tips how to avoid them. Put these strategies to work and you may reap the benefits! Don't be a financial disaster!

MISTAKE #1: HAVING NO FINANCIAL PLAN FOR THE FUTURE

When it comes to financial planning, many people have no plan. Maybe it's something we just don't think about. We tend to have very general dreams like, "One day I'd like to pay for my kids' college education," or "One day I'd like to retire." Without taking the time to set a timeline for these goals, it's very hard to accomplish anything.

Typically, when individuals initially meet with a financial planner, one of the first things they'll do is put together a list of their financial goals. While it's great to have goals written down, the problem is, they don't even know where to begin. For example, I've heard things like, "I want to retire one day to live a comfortable life," or "I want to pay for my children's education," or "I want to buy a home (or rental property or vacation home)." And the list goes on.

To tackle your goals, I recommend you incorporate a strategy to help make them attainable. You should break these goals down into different categories—short, medium, and long term, and define what those time frames mean. Then, you should categorize them into "needs," "wants," and "wishes." This strategy will help you visualize your goals and make them less overwhelming.

When you spend the time to clearly identify and separate your goals as described above, it will help you to taking these next steps. While you can certainly do them on your own, working with a credentialed professional is recommended.

1. *Figure out your spending patterns, savings plan, and investment goals.*

    • Do you have children you want to send to college? Do you have a retirement plan through work, or are you setting up your own plan? What kind of investments do you want to purchase (stocks, bonds, mutual funds, exchange traded funds)?

    • Figure out what types of accounts would be most beneficial for you and your situation.

    • Some things to consider are your age, the amount of money you can invest, the level of risk you're willing to take, and the taxes associated with different accounts.

2. *Once you have identified your goals, it's time to start working to achieve them.*

- Put these goals in writing and in a place where you can refer to them often.

- Consider reassessing your goals at least once a year, just in case you've had any major changes in your life that would require adjusting or eliminating a previous goal or adding a new one.

3. **Begin putting money aside to reach your goals, take action, and start saving!**

- Setting goals is great. But if you're not following the plan, you're wasting precious time. College and retirement might seem distant, but time goes fast and *now* is the time to start setting money aside.

- It's very easy to get into the habit of procrastinating. Many people make excuses and say money is tight this month, so they'll put money into that account next month. Guess what? They say the same thing next month too. Avoid this pattern!

4. **Motivate yourself to stay the course.**

- Once you see the big picture of your financial future, you'll probably feel a little overwhelmed at first. But more importantly, you should start to feel excited and motivated to reach your goals. Who wouldn't feel confident knowing their financial future is all planned out and looking bright? Imagine how good it will feel to get monthly or yearly statements on your accounts and see how your money is accumulating.

- Seeing positive outcomes will keep you motivated to continue on the path to financial success.

5. *Get out of debt.*

- By the time some individuals see a financial advisor, it's because they've already gotten themselves into debt and are seeking advice on how to get out. If you're in debt, you probably aren't in any financial position to be saving for college or investing in the stock market. But where will this leave you in the future?

- Maybe you're barely keeping a roof over your head. Are you wondering what you can do to make your situation better?

- Let's say you have a mortgage. Most homeowners just go on autopilot to pay it off. But what if you want to pay it off faster, and should you?

- Dreams and goals are very different. If you're daydreaming "One day I'd like to get out of debt," you may never get there. But if you actually write down "I'd like to be debt-free in fifteen years" and take action *now*, it gives you a chance to start figuring out how to get there.

When you put together a financial plan, try to stick with it for the rest of your life. Adjust it as needed, but stay with it. It's not something you just do once and forget about. Many individuals are naturally focused on the short term. That's fine as long as you're also considering the future. Our lives are dynamic and constantly changing, so making changes is normal.

While everyone is at a different stage of their life and goal planning should be customized for each individual, below is a sample of how someone might illustrate their goals.

1. **Short-term goals.** Your short-term goals are the financial issues you want to address between now and the next three years. This is the time you may want to:

   • Purchase a vehicle and obtain insurance coverage for all areas that apply (car, home, health, life, disability and long-term care).

   • Start an emergency fund.

   • Establish good credit by paying off your student loans (if you have them), being on time with your current bill payments, and not getting into debt.

   • Create a plan for savings, investments, and retirement, as well as an emergency fund. An emergency fund should have three to six months of expenses.

2. **Intermediate goals.** Your intermediate goals are those you plan to address in three to ten years. During this time, you might want to:

    •   Set aside money if you plan to get an advanced degree.

    •   Plan for wedding expenses and a down payment on a home.

    •   Prepare for the expenses associated with the birth or adoption of a child.

    •   Increase the amount of money you're saving and investing, if at all possible.

    •   Start a fund, such as a 529 plan, to provide for the college education of your children.

3. **Long-term goals.** Your long-term goals involve your financial outlook in ten years, all the way until retirement. Options like these might be in your long-term goals:

    •   Continue paying into your retirement accounts, and make housing and other plans for your retirement years.

- Plan to support aging parents and make considerations for long-term health care for them as well as for yourself and your spouse.

- Purchase investment real estate.

Once a year is a good checkpoint to ensure things are on track with your financial plan. It's like seeing your doctor once a year for a checkup. It's important to always remain proactive rather than reactive when you identify a problem.

MISTAKE #2: LIVING BEYOND YOUR MEANS

Here in America, we live in a culture of spenders. Unfortunately, we are much less a culture of savers. Are you spending 100 percent of your income each year as well as splurging on credit card purchases? If so, you're not alone!

If you are spending beyond your means, you are probably having quite a bit of trouble putting money aside or sticking to any sort of financial plan. Financial goals are based on saving money. If you're not able to save at least part of your income each month, it's hard to get anywhere.

It's hard to fix an issue until you can identify what the issue is. Therefore, start keeping track of your spending and how it relates to your income. If you're lacking a monthly cash flow analysis, that's something you should put together as soon as possible. Don't think of this as a budget, rather a method in which to track the dollars and cents that come in and out of your life each month. It is best to separate every dollar you spend and place them in categories such as household, vacation, liabilities, etc. Your "fixed" expenses will never change, such as your mortgage. The variable expenses that change each month and those that are discretionary is where you will identify ways to save.

If you're having a difficult time figuring out your spending patterns, here's an idea. Open two separate bank accounts, one for fixed expenses and another for variable. The funds deposited in the fixed expenses account will never change. Put the rest in another account and pay *all* of your variable spending for the month from that one account.

When you get your account statement at the end of the month, go line by line and look at what you're buying. See if there's anything you didn't realize you were spending, such as $100 a month on weekend entertainment.

Here's an example called "the latte factor." If you buy a latte each day, you spend approximately $5 per day. This adds up to about $150 a month. Wouldn't you be better off saving that money or using it to reach one of your financial goals?

You can really make a difference by fixing those spending habits in your cash flow. Once you have an idea of what you spend per month, you can start to identify some cost-cutting measures.

Try these ideas to cut costs to live within your means:

1. **Refinance your mortgage, auto, student, or personal loan.** Many consumers are paying a very high interest rate on their mortgage or car loan. If that applies to you, then maybe it's time to refinance.

   - If you plan to stay in your home for at least a few years, it might be well worth looking into refinancing your home at a lower interest rate. Interest rates change all the time.

   - While refinancing a home is widely popular, many aren't aware you can also refinance other loans.

   - Are you spending way too much each month on your car payment? Do you keep telling yourself your next car has to be cheaper? Have you thought about selling your car and downgrading to something less expensive? If any of these apply, think about refinancing—or even better, pay for what you can afford and don't have a loan at all!

2. **Reduce your credit card debt.** Many credit cards companies charge astronomical interest rates, especially if you have a less-than-perfect credit score. This can greatly impact your ability to ever get ahead, or even stay afloat financially. Many people get themselves into a lot of trouble with credit cards. It's the old "Credit and forget it" model!

- Call your credit card companies to try to negotiate lower finance charges, or inquire about a balance transfer from a higher interest card to a lower one.

- Start paying down your credit card debt as quickly as possible. There are two methods you can use depending on your personality.

  1. Start by paying the debt with the highest interest rate first. You have no idea how much money this will save you in the long run.

  2. The mind is powerful! Start paying the cards with the lowest balances first, regardless of interest rate. You will see how quickly you start paying it off, which will give you the confidence to start chipping away at the ones with the higher balances.

3. **Food expenses.** Dine out or eat at home? Who doesn't like a good sushi meal or a big juicy steak? Many of us like to eat out at restaurants. Some of us aren't fond of grocery shopping, cooking, or doing the dishes, which is why eating out can be appealing.

  - Have you ever kept track of how much money you spend each month by eating out? If you did, you'd probably be surprised at how quickly it adds up. Keep in mind you're probably overpaying for the food as well as paying for the service when you eat out at a restaurant.

- Designate a certain number of days each month for eating out, and stick to the plan. Imagine if you could save one or two hundred dollars per month just by eating out less.

- There are many advantages to preparing your own food. You can buy just the amount you require. Therefore, you're not paying for overpriced food or wasting costly leftovers. When you shop for food on your own, you can save money by purchasing items on sale, using coupons, selecting generic alternatives, and buying nonperishables in bulk.

- You can greatly reduce food expenses by cooking meals at home and making lunches to bring to school and work.

4. **Entertainment spending.** Everyone needs a little fun and entertainment in their lives. But sometimes things that are fun can be costly. The goal is to find less expensive alternatives to be entertained.

- If you enjoy watching television and you pay for the package with 3,000 channels, think to yourself how many of them you actually watch. With so many streaming services available, now may be time to "cut the cord." Did you know you can subscribe to a streaming service for as little as $50 per month, receive several hundred channels, and stream on multiple devices? Not only is this less expensive, but how great is it to have live television and DVR on any of your devices on demand!

- A night at the movies can be a very expensive venture. The tickets are pricey, but the concession stand is downright outrageous. If you must go to the movies, then look online for discount tickets or special offers, and bring your snacks to the theater.

5. **Household costs.** There are many different expenses associated with your home. Some of these expenses are necessary and some are a luxury. Assess your current household expenses to see where you can cut costs.

- Some of the expenses that come along with living in the digital age include cable television, phone (including cell phone), internet, video gaming, and other online-related services. Ensure you are signed up for the most economical plans available.

- Energy costs are another area of concern. Change your furnace and air conditioner filters regularly. Weather-strip drafty doors and windows. This will cut down on your energy costs for the winter. To save costs in the summer, install ceiling fans so you can circulate the air and use less air conditioning.

- To save on electricity costs, shut off lights and other electronics when they're not in use. Open your drapes during the day to take advantage of natural light. You can also use energy-efficient LED light bulbs.

- Confirm you're getting the best possible insurance rates. You might be able to choose a higher deductible on your car or homeowners insurance. See if you qualify for any discounts for a good driving record, take a driver safety course, and ask about multiline discounts (using the same insurance company for auto, home, and umbrella).

- Save money on your water bill by taking shorter showers and not running the water while you brush your teeth. Install a faucet aerator to reduce water flow without reducing pressure.

Here are some final tips for saving and managing your cash flow:

- Start by trying to save a little bit of money each day. Try to save a little each day, whatever you can manage. By the end of the month this daily savings will really add up.

- It's really scary to think, "I need to save $300 a month for my retirement. Where is that money going to come from?" But it really just comes down to $10 a day, which most of us could set aside.

- There are several good online cash flow tracking websites. One you may want to look at is Mint.com. It's a free tool you can access on your computer or with its smartphone app. It's a way to track your spending and set budgeting goals. The website also offers you advice on what you can cut from your budget as you are inputting items.

The sooner you can address your cash flow, the better. Once you get a handle on your cash flow and you learn to stick with it, you will find it much easier to live within your means.

MISTAKE #3: NOT HAVING AN EMERGENCY FUND

An emergency fund is a pool of money you can easily access when something unexpected happens. Emergency funds should be used only for major life events such as loss of a job, an illness, or a major expense needing immediate attention.

It would be nice if life always worked out as planned, but it never does. When something unexpected happens, you could suddenly find yourself unable to pay your daily or monthly expenses. An emergency fund is there so you have enough money to get you through this unexpected event and back into financial shape. As mentioned earlier, you should try to have between three to six months of expenses saved.

Many make the mistake of not setting up an emergency fund. It might be nice to think nothing bad will ever happen, or you'll be able to deal with anything that comes your way. However, life is full of surprises, and there's nothing worse than being blindsided by a tragic event.

Consider these points when starting your emergency fund:

- Saving for an emergency fund takes a bit of time, but it's one of the first financial goals you should work on.

- With a married couple, where both spouses are working, three months is probably sufficient because if one spouse loses a job, the other one is usually still working. The same applies if you're working two jobs because even if you lose one you'll likely still have the other.

- If you're a family with only one income, you should save closer to the equivalent of six months of expenses.

- A good emergency fund should focus only on paying your necessary expenses during a financial hardship. These expenses include rent or mortgage, utilities, car payment, insurance, groceries, and possibly money you owe in loans or credit card bills. One last thing to note is that there is no exact science for this. You should take into consideration all the above and plan accordingly in your emergency fund.

- Luxuries such as vacations and home imporovements should not be considered emergencies—ever. These expenses can be delayed until your financial crisis has passed.

Perhaps you've never thought about an emergency fund. Or maybe you didn't know how to start one. Start one now.

There are many ways—both traditional and creative—to build your emergency fund:

1. **Set a goal for starting your emergency fund.** After you decide how much you spend each month and how many months you want to have saved in your emergency fund, it's time to break it down.

    - Figure out how much you can contribute each month. Then you'll know how long it will take to build up that amount.

    - It might be a good idea to set up automatic payments that take money from your main checking account and put it into your emergency fund savings account. When it happens automatically, it's one less thing for you to address.

- Once you reach your goal amount, you can then decide if you want to build it further (the cost of expenses for another three to six months), or if you want to allocate that money elsewhere.

2. **Start small.**

- *Even if you have little to save at first, that's okay.* The important thing is to not delay any longer.

- Maybe you'll only be able to contribute $20 per paycheck at the start. But that's better than nothing. Stay positive! Eventually, you'll be able to add more. As you see your emergency fund grow, you'll get motivated to try and save more.

3. **Contribute "wasted" money to your emergency fund.**

- Look for any possible "money leaks" in your cash flow. Watch your spending and live within your means.

- Get your entire family involved by saving spare change. Find a jar or jug and put it in a central location. When family members arrive home each day, have them empty the spare change from their pockets or purses into the jug. At the end of the month, take the money and deposit it into your emergency fund.

4.   **Save your tax refunds or bonus check.**

- If you're fortunate enough to get a yearly bonus at work or hefty tax refund, be smart with your money. Instead of spending your bonus or tax refund on a fancy vacation or frivolous expense, why not deposit it into your emergency fund? Think about how quickly it could add up.

An emergency fund can be the difference between financial success and financial failure. Which category do you want to fall into?

Set up an emergency fund now so you won't be caught off guard when an unforeseen event occurs. One disastrous financial setback could unravel everything else you've been saving for.

MISTAKE #4: WAITING TOO LONG TO START SAVING FOR RETIREMENT

Although retirement seems far off, it's actually closer than you think. Some people will spend more time in retirement than they did in their working years! Therefore, the earlier you can start saving for retirement, the better.

Here are a few steps to help prepare you for retirement:

1.   **Start planning for retirement.** As with many other financial aspects, it's important to create a plan.

- Start saving as soon as you possibly can. Again, it's okay to start out small if necessary. Just figure out what you can afford to contribute and continue to increase the amount whenever possible.

- Do some research! Start looking into different types of retirement accounts.

2. **Learn about retirement savings plans through your employer.** Find out what types of retirement savings plans are available at work.

   - If your company offers a retirement plan such as a 401(k), sign up immediately and start contributing all you can. Your contributions will be automatically deducted, and your income taxes will be lower. Tax deferrals, account growth, and compound interest is powerful.

   - If a 401(k) is offered, find out if your company pays anything into this fund or if they'll match your contributions. Ask how much you would need to contribute to get the full employer contribution and how long you're required to stay with the plan in order to get that money. At the minimum, you should always contribute up to the employer match.

   - Maybe your employer offers a traditional pension plan instead. See if you're eligible to be covered under this plan. Learn how it works. Ask for a benefit statement so you can keep track of your pension.

- Find out what will happen to your retirement benefits if you end up changing jobs before you retire.

3. **Begin putting money into an individual retirement account (IRA).** Whether you have other retirement accounts, you can always start your own IRA. These types of retirement accounts are offered by many financial institutions.

- For 2020, you can put up to $6,000 ($7,000 if you are age fifty or older) into an IRA. You can also start with much less if you want, but there are tax advantages to consider.

- There are two main types of IRAs. In a tradtional IRA, the money is not taxed initially, but is taxed as income when it's withdrawn at retirement. In a Roth IRA, the money is taxed initially and there are no additional taxes when you withdraw.

4. **Consider other investment opportunities.** Setting up IRAs, 401(k)s, and other pension plans are great ways to start. However, you should also consider other investment opportunities.

- The money in your retirement accounts is invested in different ways. For example, if a company offers a 401(k) to its employees, the company plan usually provides its own limited "menu" of investments you can choose. With an IRA, you have more investment choices, including certificates of deposit (CDs), mutual funds, stocks, and bonds.

- Carefully track your investments so you can rearrange them if you aren't happy with how they're performing. You should be putting your retirement savings in many different types of investments. Diversifying in this way contributes to growth and reduces risk. *Note: There is no guarantee that a diversified portfolio will enhance overall returns or out-perform a non-diversified portfolio. Diversification does not protect against market risk.*

- You can also open investment accounts that are not retirement accounts. A regular brokerage account opened with post-tax dollars is another way to grow your assets. These are often referred to as nonqualified accounts.

5. **Find out about Social Security benefits.** Social Security is a system set up by the government to assist retirees after they have stopped working. These monetary benefits are paid on a monthly basis to those who paid into the system before they retired.

- This system was never meant to be the sole source of income for retirees. Social Security replaces only about 40 percent of the average income. More than likely you'll probably need 70 to 90 percent of your preretirement income to live comfortably.

- Social Security money helps, but retirees should draw from other retirement accounts, private pensions, savings, and investments upon retirement.

- Social Security benefits are taxable in line with one's income level. If you're a single taxpayer with an income above $25,000, or a married couple with an income above $32,000, your Social Security benefits may be taxed.

- Even if a wife has never earned an income, under Social Security she may be able to get benefits if she is at least sixty-two years old and if her husband is eligible to receive retirement benefits.

- Some financial analysts predict the funds in the Social Security system will be depleted in the upcoming years. Nobody knows for sure, but being prepared in other ways is the best defense against this possible tragedy.

- Social Security is a complicated system, and there are many choices to make when it's time to start collecting. You should seek the advice of a specialist to help maximize your benefit amount.

An Example

Let's work through an example, using the retirement calculator at Bloomberg.com to help you figure out your retirement savings.

Here's the question. How much do you have to save per month to have $1 million by age sixty-five?

If you start at age twenty-five, to get $1 million at sixty-five you need to save less than $200 a month in order to save $1 million by age sixty-five. This is probably doable for most people.

If you start at age thirty-five, to hit the same goal you need to save $500 a month, which is more than double. This may be more difficult, but if you have a good job and are well-established, this is also possible.

If you don't start saving until you're forty-five years of age, you would need to put aside $1,500 a month in order to reach that $1 million goal. That's why it's very difficult when people wait until they're forty-five to start saving for retirement.

It's Never Too Late to Start Saving

What if you're in your forties or fifties and haven't started saving for retirement yet? First of all, stay positive! Although the above example may have looked bleak, anything you can do now is better than nothing. At this point, you'll probably just have to adjust your retirement goals.

Instead of retiring at sixty-five, maybe you'll have to work until you're seventy. The amount of your retirement fund will be less too. You won't be able to reach $1 million unless you have $1,500 per month to put away. You might have to settle for a retirement income of $35,000 to $40,000 per year.

Nevertheless, it's never too late to start saving. If you're forty-five years old, get started immediately. You'll be in much better shape than the person who started at fifty-five. The sooner you start putting money aside, the sooner you'll start putting that money to work for you.

It's more important than ever to plan for your own retirement. Social Security could be in danger. In this economy, many companies no longer offer pension plans, and others have stopped matching 401(k) contributions.

You can't afford to put off saving for retirement! Try to find a way to start saving even $100 a month and put it into a retirement plan like an IRA or a 401(k), or even just put it in a regular nonqualified investment account. As you can see, it really adds up.

MISTAKE #5: NOT ENOUGH INSURANCE

Not having enough insurance coverage is another common issue. This most commonly occurs with life insurance.

Many of us aren't happy about having to buy insurance coverage. There's nothing fun about spending money on something you hope you'll never have to use. However, nobody can afford to be without insurance if something catastrophic does happen. If you ever actually have an incident where you use your insurance, you'll find it more than makes up for the cost.

You can think of insurance as being similar to an emergency fund, but it's specified for a certain type of emergency. If you lack adequate insurance, it can seriously derail your financial well-being.

When talking about insurance, the subject of liability insurance is important to address. Liability insurance is what you get with your auto and homeowners policies. If someone gets injured as a result of something you did and they sue you, your liability insurance will cover the damages.

You want to have your liability coverage equal to your net worth, because someone could sue you for that amount of money.

Here's where you can get in trouble. Let's say you have $300,000 worth of assets and only $150,000 worth of liability coverage on your auto policy. If you injured someone and get hit with a lawsuit, you could end up losing $150,000.

Check your liability limits to ensure you are at the correct level. If your coverage is lacking, it should be quick and fairly inexpensive to increase it to an acceptable level. That said, having an umbrella policy could rectify the shortfall.

Other than not having a sufficient amount of insurance coverage, it's also important to maintain several *types* of insurance.

These types of insurance are critical to protect your financial nest egg:

1. **Health insurance.** Health insurance is probably the most important type of insurance you can have. Health care costs are astronomical, and one illness or hospitalization could drain your savings account to nothing.

   • You might be surprised to know one of the leading reasons why people declare bankruptcy is because they got sick or injured and were without health insurance.

   • If you don't already have insurance, check with your employer. Most companies offer individual and family health insurance to their employees at fairly affordable prices.

   • If you're self-employed or your place of employment doesn't offer health insurance, then you must seek health insurance on your own.

   • If you plan to use your health insurance often, you want a low deductible and copays. If you rarely see a doctor, you can shop around for plans with higher deductibles and copays, as they'll save you money on your premium.

- Although the cost may seem like a financial burden, the potential cost of not having health insurance coverage is too high to risk.

2. **Homeowners insurance.** The idea of having to replace your home is an expensive and scary thought. It's vital to protect your home and valuables inside against theft and damage. Homeowners insurance is essential in safeguarding you and your home.

- When you have a mortgage, homeowners insurance can be a requirement of your lender. Sometimes, the cost of your insurance premium is built into your mortgage payment.

- When looking for a homeowners policy, be certain it covers three things: the replacement of the structure, the belongings inside your house, and the cost of living elsewhere while your house is being repaired. Quick tip: if you don't have receipt for expensive valuables in your home, take pictures of the items and store them in a safe place or in the cloud.

- A regular homeowners insurance policy may not be enough to fully protect your home. You may require additional coverage for fire, earthquakes, tornadoes, flooding, and other potential disasters.

- You also want your homeowners policy to cover any liability should someone get injured while they're at your house or on your property. This is similar to the above example regarding the auto accident.

- If you're renting instead, there is a different policy for you. Similar to a homeowners policy, renters insurance covers you against theft or damage to your personal items. Renters insurance is an affordable way to recover the replacement costs of your belongings should there be a burglary, fire, or other disaster.

3. **Auto insurance.** Auto insurance protects car owners in many ways. In most states, auto insurance is required by law. Still, many drivers still get behind the wheel without it, which is very risky on many levels.

- Your car is another of your more pricey possesions. If it gets damaged, you want to be able to repair or replace it.

- Even more important than replacing the car is taking care of any treatments for injuries sustained by the drivers or passengers. As previously mentioned, health-related services are costly, making this type of coverage a necessity.

- If you're involved in an accident without being insured, you could be subject to a lawsuit that could cost you everything you own in order to pay for property damage and injury or death of an involved party.

- There are many facets to car insurance: comprehensive, personal injury protection, collision, uninsured motorist, and liability. It's good to discuss your needs in these areas with your insurance agent.

- If you have an older car, you may choose only the minimum level of liability insurance. However, if you have a newer car, especially one with a high value, you may want to carry a comprehensive plan with additional coverage against theft.

- Some auto insurance policies also cover legal defense costs in case you end up in court after your car accident.

4. **Umbrella insurance.** Umbrella insurance is extra insurance that provides protection beyond existing limits and coverages of your other policies. It can provide coverage for injuries, property damage, certain lawsuits, and personal liability situations.

- Despite what you may think, umbrella coverage is not that expensive.

- The purpose is to cover claims that exceed your other basic policy liability limits. This could include homeowners, auto, or watercraft.

- Not only will the policy cover the pollicyholder but also other members of the family or household.

5. **Life insurance.** Life insurance protects those who are financially dependent on you.

   - If you're the breadwinner and your spouse, children, or parents would face a financial hardship if you passed away, then life insurance should be a top priority.

   - Life insurance helps provide a cushion to offset any lost income the deceased no longer earns, as well as pays for the fees associated with a funeral.

   - In order to figure how much life insurance coverage you should have, look at your yearly earnings and multiply by the number of years you plan to remain employed. Factor in burial costs to determine an appropriate amount for your situation.

   - Let's say you buy a policy for $500,000, which may seem like plenty. But when you break it down, it barely covers anything. If you were given a check for $500,000, could you live off that and never work again? Probably not. That's why this policy is insufficient.

- Many life insurance policies cover pretty large amounts. It's not uncommon to purchase one million dollars or more in coverage.

- Check with your employer to see if life insurance benefits are offered. If so, it is usually inexpensive. Even if you have your own policy, consider what's offered by your employer a bonus.

Other Types of Insurance Policies

There are also other types of insurance you may want to consider.

Business insurance. If you own a business, you may want to invest in business insurance. This type of policy protects against any business-related losses. Business insurance usually covers things such as legal liability, employee-related issues, and property damage.

Unfortunately, we live in a litigious society. For example, if a customer gets hurt on the premises of your business, they could take you to court and go after both your business and personal assets. That's why business owners can't be without this sort of protection.

What is your most valuable asset? Did you say your house? If you did, that's what most people think. What if you couldn't go to work and earn an income to pay your mortgage, taxes, and other obligations? Shift your mindset—perhaps your most valuable asset is *you*! It's your ability to get up every day and earn a living.

Disability insurance. This type of insurance is important if you ever get injured or sick and can no longer work. Disability insurance should cover most of your salary. The majority of insurance companies will allow you to cover up to 60 percent of your salary. If you pay the premiums using after-tax dollars, the benefit is paid to you tax-free. In this instance, the tax-free benefit would cover almost all of your taxable salary.

Disability policies can be used for temporary, permanent, partial, or total disability. For example, what if you were in a serious car accident and could never work again? Most of us could not afford to be off work for a prolonged period of time without some sort of money coming in. Disability insurance provides that monetary compensation.

Some disability policies can be expensive. But perhaps you can find one that is affordable for you. The cost may actually be worth it. You may pay far less for the insurance now than it would cost if something happened and you were left with no money at all.

Long term care. This insurance policy will help cover an individual's expenses when they need help doing basic activities of daily living such as eating, bathing, and dressing.

Do You Really Need Long-Term Care Insurance?

One of the largest medical costs you may incur in your lifetime is long-term care. For care outside of the home, a private room in a nursing home or assisted living facility can cost over $75,000 a year. Long-term care insurance, while not cheap, can reduce that burden.

The biggest criticism of these policies has been their cost. However, this insurance can save you a tremendous amount of money in medical expenses, and ultimately protect the assets you worked so hard to accumulate.

How Can You Compare Quotes?

Insurance is a competitive market. It's not a bad idea to do research online about the types of policies that exist and the benefits of each. Premiums could range from company to company, but it's always important to make sure you do a true "apples to apples" comparison. What may appear as the same coverage could have minor differences that change the premium amounts. Knowing what each policy has to offer will help you make your decision.

You should also do research on the insurance companies themselves. You want to choose an insurance company that has a high rating and a positive claims history.

The agent selling you these policies should also be vetted. Some insurance agents are considered "captive" and can sell only the insurance company they represent. There are insurance agents who offer multiple carriers and can help you choose the best one for your situation. This is true for most types of insurance, whether it be auto, home, life, etc

Note: Please keep in mind that insurance companies alone determine insurability and some people may be deemed uninsurable becasue of health reasons, occupation, and lifestyle choices. Guarantees are based on the claims paying ability of the issuing company.

MISTAKE #6: NAMING MINORS AS BENEFICIARIES—OR YOUR ESTATE

Sometimes an honest, well-intentioned gesture could have severe consequences. When you apply for a life insurance policy, enroll in your company retirement plan, or complete an IRA application, you may be inclined to name your minor children as beneficiaries. This is one of the most common mistakes people make.

A financial institution will not write a check made payable to a minor. In most states, the age of majority is eighteen. Assuming you did name a minor child as your beneficiary and you passed away, here is most likely what will happen. First, even if you are married, your spouse would have to petition the courts to be appointed a guardian until your child becomes the age of the majority. This could be a lengthy and costly ordeal. Once this happens, assuming at age eighteen, your child would become the rightful owner of those proceeds. Imagine what an eighteen-year-old would do with all that money. If you were not married, or if you are married and died in a common accident, this scenario become much worse. The death of a parent(s) is hard enough, let alone now having to embark on a potential legal battle among family members or friends.

So, what do you do if you want to ensure your children are properly cared for financially? One, you can utilize your state's Uniformed Transfers to Minor's Act (UTMA) laws and name an adult custodian to receive the proceeds for the benefit of the child. The custodian will have the authority to use the proceeds to care for the minor children. Each state law is slightly different, so you want to make sure to verify the specific language in your state. While this does prevent court intervention initially, it doesn't stop the child from receiving the full amount when they turn the age of majority.

A trust is not just created for the rich! There are many types of trusts that exist, and many of them can be funded with life insurance and other assets. Having a trust allows you to dictate how you want your money spent from the grave. When a trust is created, you would name someone you trust to act as a trustee (spouse, family member, friend). This person would carry out your wishes as to how and when your child should receive money. The trustee must act in a fiduciary capacity to ensure your children are taken care of financially in a prudent manner. Trusts should also be used when you have a child or dependent with special needs. Many individuals who have special needs receive government assistance. A person receiving money from a government program risks losing their benefits if that person were to inherit money over a certain limit. These limits are negligible.

One benefit of products that offer beneficiary designations is that they avoid the probate process. Upon death, a beneficiary could receive proceeds fairly quickly. All too often when a person leaves a beneficiary designation blank, the default becomes your estate. In other instances, some will actually name their estate as a beneficiary. This again can cause many issues, such as probate, family feuds, and potentially unnecessary taxes due.

The moral of this mistake is to carefully choose your beneficiaries and never name minor children, even as contingents. If you are unsure of how to complete beneficiary forms or uncertain which of your financial products are beneficiary eligible, you should seek the advice of a professional.

CONCLUSION

Your financial future should never be neglected. Money can't buy happiness, but it does buy you the necessities to live a comfortable life. Financial mistakes can hold you back from living the life you deserve. Try not to follow in the footsteps of those who have made financial blunders.

If you lack a financial plan for the future, then make one today. If you're living outside your means, it's time to assess your spending, cut out unnecessary expenses, create a cash flow model, and stick to it.

Nobody wants to endure an emergency. However, you should expect the unexpected. Set up an emergency fund and be ready with the money needed to handle a crisis.

Most individuals look forward to retirement. Start saving for retirement right now! You will work hard for many years, and retirement is your special time to enjoy. Ensure you have the means to sustain your living expenses when you no longer work.

Last, but not least, purchase a sufficient amount of insurance coverage. If something happens to your health, car, home, or life, you'll be glad you did.

SIX COSTLY MISTAKES WORKSHEET

MISTAKE #1: HAVING NO FINANCIAL PLAN FOR THE FUTURE

1. List the financial areas you would like to research.

   _____

   _____

   _____

2. How will you begin putting money aside to reach your goals? Be specific.

   _____

   _____

   _____

3. List three ways you can motivate yourself to take action toward reaching your financial goals.

   _____

   _____

   _____

   _____

4. What is your plan to get out of debt? List your debts here and then write your plan.

_____

_____

_____

5. Short-term financial goals. What are your financial goals for the next three years?

_____

_____

_____

6. Intermediate financial goals. What goals do you plan to address in three to ten years?

_____

_____

_____

7. Long-term financial goals. Starting with ten years from now to retirement, what will you work on?

_____

_____

_____

_____

MISTAKE #2: LIVING OUTSIDE YOUR MEANS

8. What adjustments in your daily living can you make now to cut costs? What will you do beginning this week, this month, and this year?

_____

_____

_____

_____

MISTAKE #3: NOT HAVING AN EMERGENCY FUND

9. Set a goal for the date you'll start saving for your emergency fund, and put it here.

_____

_____

_____

_____

10. How much will you save and how often?

_____

_____

_____

_____

11. List at least three ways you waste money during the week and how much. That could be money you put into your emergency fund.

1. _____

2. _____

3. _____

12. Record here any tax refunds or employment bonuses this year, and put them here. These could be used toward your emergency fund or other savings (i.e., other investments or retirement fund).

_____

_____

_____

MISTAKE #4: WAITING TOO LONG TO START SAVING FOR RETIREMENT

13. What can you do to investigate retirement accounts?

_____

_____

_____

_____

_____

14. Do you already have a retirement account? If not, call your employer or a financial advisor to inquire about such plans. Start one by the end of this month, if possible. Write notes below.

_____

_____

_____

15. Check into your future Social Security benefits this week. Go online to the Social Security website at www.ssa.gov to research your benefits. Write what you learned below. If you need to call them with your questions, the number is 1-800-772-1213.

_____

_____

_____

MISTAKE #5: NOT ENOUGH INSURANCE

16. List all your insurance policies. Include payout limits and benefits on each.

Health insurance

_____

_____

_____

Homeowners or renters insurance

_____

Auto insurance

_____

Life insurance

_____

Other insurances

_____

17. What insurance do you need that you don't already have? Or, do you have policies you need to review to ensure you have enough coverage? If so, list them here.

_____

_____

_____

_____

_____

_____

_____

18. If you require insurance quotes, try to get at least two quotes for each type of insurance you think you need. Write the details about premium payments and coverage benefits so you can make the best decisions for your circumstances.

_____

_____

_____

_____

_____

MISTAKE #6: NAMING MINORS OR YOUR ESTATE AS BENEFICIARIES

19. Make sure you have gone through all accounts that require beneficiaries and none of them have minors listed as either primary or contingents. If you need do change anything, you can list them here.

_____

_____

_____

_____

_____

Be vigilant about how you manage your money in order to pursue financial independence!

FINANCIAL MYTHS: EXPOSED!

Financial advice is often given via many different mediums—turn on the television, listen to a radio show, surf the internet, or listen to a podcast, coworker down the hall, your family member at the dinner table, etc. But how do you know what's actually true? It is possible some of the ideas, concepts, products might pertain to you, but there's a good chance they may not. Each and every person has a unique situation, and therefore must take action based upon their specific circumstance. Throughout my decades of experience as a financial professional, I've heard many clients and "talking heads" make statements and suggestions that I consider myths. Below you will find several of them I will intelligently rebut.

I am too old to start planning.

While it is certainly ideal to start saving as soon as you are able, it really is never too late. Having something is certainly better than having nothing. The challenge you face as you age, is the need to save a greater amount in a shorter period of time. On a positive note, you may have more time than you think. Assuming you are forty-five years old and haven't started saving for retirement, you still have a good twenty years to save. With the power of compound interest, you would be surprised to see how quickly it adds up. As a hypothetical example, if you were to start saving $1,000 per month starting at age forty-five for twenty years at 6 percent, you would have $462,041 by age 65. As you can see, consistent saving at a decent rate of return certainly helps. That said, going from nothing to playing "catch-up" will take serious discipline and potentially some lifestyle changes.

Estate planning is only for the wealthy.

In February 2020, the world lost one of the most famous sports icons in history, Kobe Bryant, his daughter, and seven others in a tragic helicopter crash. Mr. Bryant was only forty-one years old. While Mr. Bryant had significant wealth, this situation reminds us of the importance of ensuring our loved ones are taken care of financially.

Do you have a will? If your answer is no, you are actually wrong! You may never have signed your name to an actual legal document; however, every person does in fact have a "built-in" default will. This plan is called *dying intestate*. When you die intestate, without a will that you have signed and executed, the court system will ultimately decide your financial fate, making other important decisions that might arise. A will dictates how your assets and property will be divided when you pass away. These assets may be as simple as a basic checking or savings account. In addition, a will can outline guardianship for minor children.

In 2005 the country witnessed a famous right-to-die case involving a woman named Terri Schiavo. Ms. Schiavo didn't have any executed advanced directives (living will). Her case faced legal challenges for several years in the court system, and President George W. Bush was even involved. Her husband's argument was that he knew his wife would've never wanted to live in a vegetative state, while her parents took the opposite position. A seven-year battle ultimately led to removing Ms. Schiavo from life support. Don't let something like this happen to you.

Having even the most basic estate-planning documents in place will prevent family legal battles and ensure your instructions are followed at your death. While a very difficult and emotional process, it's one that is necessary no matter how much or how little wealth you have.

I need life insurance only temporarily to care for my minor children and/or to pay off my mortgage.

When I was sixteen years old my grandmother passed away. Four years earlier, she was diagnosed with breast cancer that ultimately spread to her brain. The doctors explained that her condition was terminal, but they couldn't specify how long she had left. My grandfather was sixty-six years old at the time and had recently retired with a nest egg that would last for the rest of his life. I remember my grandparents having the most loving relationship of anyone I had ever met. My grandfather made it his mission to extend her life for as long as possible. Within two years, my grandfather had just about spent his entire nest egg caring for my grandmother, and when she died he had almost nothing left. At age sixty-seven he returned to the workforce so he was able to sustain his own lifestyle, as Social Security was certainly not enough.

You may be thinking long-term care could've helped, and you would be correct. That said, he didn't have that, either. Life is full of unknowns, and nobody knows what they may be, which is why planning is so important. Assuming for a moment my grandmother didn't suffer from a health-related disease that prevented her from performing activities of daily living (that long-term care would cover), it's possible the same economic devastation could've occurred for a different reason.

If my grandfather had a life insurance policy on my grandmother, upon death the death benefit would've served as a replacement to the money he had spent for her care.

There are many types of life insurance policies that could stay in effect for someone's entire life, which is discussed later in this book. Unlike the situation above, there are so many other reasons why someone may need or want life insurance for their entire life—for example, to cover estate taxes, multigenerational wealth transfer, single life pension replacement, etc.

Every person's situation is different and needs to be examined carefully and should be well thought out. While these types of policies may not be for everyone, the myth of buying life insurance only while your children are young, or to cover a mortgage or other debts, is simply not true.

When I retire, I'll be in a lower tax bracket.

Here's what I would like you to do right now. Put this book down, take out a blank piece of paper and a pen, and write down all the reasons you think taxes will go down in the future. Is there anything written on your paper? Mine is blank! Now, I want you to repeat the same exercise but write down why you think taxes will go up in the future. Which list is larger?

Retirement is considered your "golden years." It's the time for you to really enjoy the "fruit of the vine." You worked for years saving toward reaching a retirement that would be fulfilling, enjoyable, and fun. If you maintain a certain lifestyle today, do you really want to change that lifestyle when you retire? If anything, you may want to spend more on things like travel, a second residence, golf, or other entertainment, nice meals with friends and family, etc. All of these cost money. There has never been a single client who has come to my office who told me they want to spend less money during retirement and cut back on all the things they enjoy doing.

With strategic planning, you are more than likely facing a similar or higher tax bracket when you retire. That said, while maximizing 401(k) contributions is not "bad," and you receive a tax deduction for the contribution, upon distribution it will be taxed at ordinary income tax rates. Understanding this concept is critical when deciding where to allocate every dollar available to save.

Never ever buy an annuity.

If you are a frequent CNBC watcher, you may have seen the commercial from a well-known money manager (to remain nameless) who says, "I would die and go to hell before I bought an annuity." This blanket statement is just wrong! The truth is, annuities have received a plethora of bad press through the years. Not because they are bad products, but because either the wrong type of annuity is sold, or it's not beneficial to the person making the purchase.

The offering of pensions by corporations is becoming less frequent. They are expensive to fund and maintain, and therefore are becoming extinct. Many modern-day annuities offer living benefit riders, which help provide a guaranteed income stream during retirement. In essence, the insurance companies design these products to act as a replacement vehicle for pensions. If they are used correctly with a person who understands how they can be properly integrated with an overall planning strategy, they can be extremely worthwhile and advantageous.

You must be rich to invest.

Perhaps you think only doctors, lawyers, trust-fund babies, or businessmen invest in the stock market. This line of thinking is just flat-out false! With interest rates as low as they are today and not too many places to save, you are potentially leaving huge amounts of money on the table. Even the smallest amount invested in the stock market can make a difference. When I say small, I mean it—even pennies a day! When Apple announced the invention of the Apple App Store, its famous quote was, "There's an app for that." Well, there is an app for saving literally pennies a day for stocks. There are apps that will connect to your bank account debit card, and after each purchase, round up to the nearest dollar and place those remaining cents into stocks! Yes, this really is true. There are several variations of this, but two you might want to check out are Acorns and Robinhood.

Carry a small credit card balance to increase your credit score.

This can't be further from the truth. Your credit score is calculated in several different ways, and carrying balances is one of them. The amount of debt you carry will impact your score and the amount banks are willing to lend. If you use credit cards to make purchases, you should pay off your balances in full each month. This activity will have a positive effect on your credit score, not by carrying a balance.

I should take Social Security as soon as I'm eligible.

Social Security benefits could become a main source of income once you retire. It is important to understand how these benefits work, figure out the best time to file, and know how much you'll receive on a monthly basis. Just choosing to take Social Security when you are eligible could leave you missing out on tens of thousands of dollars. Below are answers to some very common questions.

Who qualifies for Social Security benefits?

Qualification is based on a credit system. You need to earn a total of forty credits during your life. You can earn up to four credits a year, and one credit is awarded every time you meet a certain earning requirement. This amount varies from one year to the next. You will become eligible for Social Security benefits if you met earning requirements for a total of ten years.

How are benefits calculated?

Only the thirty-five years during which you earned the most are considered. An average is then calculated to figure out what a typical income was during these thirty-five years. An index is used to adjust this income to account for inflation. If you wait until full retirement age to file for benefits, you'll receive the full amount of your benefits based on these thirty-five years.

What is full retirement age?

Your full retirement age depends on your birth date. For those born from 1943 to 1954, the full retirement age is sixty-six. The full retirement age creeps upward, and those born in 1960 or later can receive full benefits at age sixty-seven. It's important to note your full retirement age, since waiting only a couple of months before you file for benefits could make a difference in how much you receive.

Can you get benefits before you reach full retirement age?

You can start collecting your Social Security benefits once you reach the age of sixty-two, but you will only get a portion of what your benefits would be if you waited until you reached age sixty-six or sixty-seven. If you decide to file early, your payments from Social Security are reduced a bit for each year before your full retirement age.

Can you delay receiving benefits?

You can choose when you start receiving Social Security benefits. Your benefits will continue to increase past your full retirement age if you do not file right away. They will increase by 8 percent for each year that you wait.

How can you file for Social Security benefits?

All you have to do is visit the official Social Security website at ssa.gov and create an account. The filing process is pretty straightforward, but it is recommended to start the application process at least three months in advance.

You'll probably have to upload some documents such as your tax returns, marriage certificate, and birth certificate. Preparing all these documents in advance will definitely speed up the approval process.

Can you find out how much your benefits will be in advance?

You can create an account on ssa.gov even if you don't plan on applying for benefits at the moment. This will give you access to helpful information such as the amount of your benefits. In the end, the benefits you'll receive depend on how much money you earned during your life, when you file for benefits, and how long you live.

For an average life expectancy, you'll end up receiving about the same total benefits regardless of when you file. You can receive less money for a longer period of time, or more money for a shorter period of time. You get to decide which works best for you.

I don't need a financial advisor, I can do it myself.

Today you decide to take a walk to get some fresh air. As you are strolling down the block, you trip on a sharp object and cut your leg. The gash on your shin is so deep, you need stitches. You jump in your car, head over to the nearest medical supply store, and buy everything you need to stitch yourself up. Wait, is this something you would really do?

There is certainly nothing stopping you from doing your own planning, but is it smart? A good financial advisor stays current with changes in the tax code, understands all the different types of investment vehicles, is proficient in insurance, etc.

You need a plan to help you achieve your goals, and a financial advisor will help you with just that. It is recommended you find a financial advisor who is acting in fiduciary capacity. This means they are working for your sole benefit and not their own. You should rely on this professional to give you sound advice, build a plan, and speak with any other professionals who may guide you, like a CPA or attorney. Work with an advisor who takes a "team" approach with those other professionals so each professional understands their role and the team can work to help you.

One last tip that has been mentioned before—find an advisor who has a planning designation such as a Certified Financial Planner (CFP®) or Chartered Financial Consultant (ChFC®).

I don't have enough money to start saving.

Saving money is as much a product of the mind as well as your financial habits. And speaking of habits, you'll see how making small, positive changes turned into habits, can automatically add up to big savings!

1. Track your spending. Record every penny you spend for a month. Divide your spending reports into categories, such as restaurants, groceries, entertainment, clothing, house payment, utilities, and other categories. You might be surprised to learn where all your money went!

    •   At the end of a month, analyze your reports. Identify areas where you could cut down. Next month, cut down on those expenses and put the money you saved into your savings.

2. Clarify wants versus needs. There are certain things in life that you need to survive, such as food, water, clothing, and shelter. There are also the things that you want. Learn to differentiate between the two, and you'll automatically make some choices that will save you money.

3. Buy only what you can afford. You may think that you have to get every new gadget and gizmo available, but if you cannot afford them, the financial struggles they cause will outweigh the enjoyment that you receive from them.

    •   Consider using the cash envelope method of planning for your spending. Divide your expenses into categories and use a different envelope for each category. With each paycheck, divide your money into the various envelopes.

- Spend only the money that you've planned for each category. Once the cash is gone, it's gone until more money can be added to that envelope.

- You may want to save for a few weeks to get enough cash in your envelope for a desired purchase, at which time you'll know that you can afford it.

4. Do you need that new shiny, expensive car? If you're struggling each month to repay the high-interest loan that you had to take out to pay for your car, perhaps you'll want to rethink whether you need such an expensive car.

- In some situations, you might need an expensive car. For example, if you're a real estate agent and you take clients to look at high-end houses for sale, an expensive, luxury car might help you make sales. This assumes you can afford it.

- On the other hand, in reflection, if you bought the car to impress the neighbors, you might feel that the additional expense and resulting financial struggles aren't really worth it. If this is the case, a downgrade to an attractive, less expensive car may work better for you.

- Consider what a car is really for: to get you from one place to another, usually for short jaunts within your city. A less expensive car can get you there as well as a high-end car. Plus, you'll have the extra money to do with as you please.

5. If you have too much room in your house, perhaps it's time to consider downsizing. A smaller home can save tens of thousands of dollars on the purchase price and monthly payment. Plus, costs for maintenance and repairs are less. Even if you rent, a smaller place will likely cost less.

- Imagine the amount of money that you could save with a smaller house! All this money can then be used for other things that are important to you, like vacations, or to add to your savings for retirement.

- Downsizing is an important decision that only you can make. Decide what's more important to you—the larger house or the savings. For example, you might need extra room because you frequently have guests. An office space might be vital to the success of your business.

- Figure out if downsizing might work for you, and, if so, go for it!

6. Figure out ways in which you can enjoy life while still saving money. Money does not dictate how much you enjoy life. Remember, it's not the material things in your life that matter most, but rather your friends, family, and the cherished times you have with each other.

    - Research shows that the experiences in our life bring greater happiness than material items.

    - For example, instead of going out to dinner and a movie, invite your friends over for a potluck dinner and movie night at your house. You can still enjoy a rollicking good evening together while saving money. You might even enjoy it more than sitting in the restaurant and theater!

    - There are many other ways to substitute something less expensive and still have fun, like game night, sports (playing volleyball, basketball, baseball, football, soccer, bowling), card games, going camping or to the beach, and more.

    - Create your own list of activities that are fun for you that don't cost a lot of money. Invite your friends to do the same, and then choose those activities whenever you want to get together. You'll all have fun and save money too!

7. Adopt some small, financially savvy habits, such as:

- **Save first.** Automatically have a small amount of each paycheck deposited into your savings. You won't miss what you never see!

- **Let your money work for you.** Invest regularly so that money will grow by itself into more money! Over the years, this can add up to many thousands or tens of thousands more than what you put in.

- **Cook at home most of the time.** Saving money by cutting down on fast food and coffee runs will add up.

- **Buy when things are on sale.** Try to avoid ever paying full price.

- **Use free or streaming services for watching television.** You can likely get the entertainment you want for a much smaller price, and pocket substantial savings.

Saving money doesn't have to be a burden. Try these tips, and you'll find that you'll actually have more money for the things you really want in life!

The stock market is facing a crisis, so I should sell, sit on cash, and wait for the rebound! Or the opposite—the market is at an all-time high and is about to crash, so I should sell now.

It's every investor's dream to time the market. PhDs in finance and mathematics toil away at market simulations. However, no one has ever developed a system of timing the market that proved to be successful. The variables involved are too complex and the impact of human-driven factors is too high.

Avoid listening to the financial pundits who claim today is a great day or a bad day to get in or out of the market. If they were consistently correct, they wouldn't bother telling you. Instead, they'd be off adding to their billions.

CONSIDER THESE IDEAS:

1. Anyone who could accurately predict short-term changes in the market would find himself among the richest people in the world. There are plenty of wealthy investors, but few of them got that way by predicting short-term changes in the market.

    - There are wealthy investors who became wealthy by taking long-term positions.

    - Hedge fund managers and mutual fund managers are wealthy, but they get paid whether they perform well or not.

- A few short-term investors have made it big, but they lose money more frequently than they make money. A few big gains can offset multiple losses. It's a crapshoot.

- In short, no one has consistently done well timing the market. You're unlikely to be the first.

2. You miss out on too much. When most people try to time the market, they get out too soon. Eventually the market falls, but then they wait too long to get back in. You also face a high opportunity cost. While you're sitting around waiting, your money isn't doing much. Studies have shown that it's more lucrative to stay in the market than to jump in and out.

- Missing out on just a couple of good days has been proven to be a significant disadvantage. From 1993 to 2013, the S&P rose by an average of 9.2 percent each year. If you missed out on the ten best days that year, your annual return would only be 5.4 percent. It's not just the gains you miss. It's the compounding from those gains that you miss out on.

3. The fees (commissions) associated with buying and selling can add up if you don't have a fee-only managed account. Depending on how many stocks you own, you could be losing money each time you buy and sell. Can you gain enough from timing the

market to offset these additional costs and the tax hit? Nope.

4. Each time you sell and take your gains, you're forced to pay taxes on those earnings. That means you have less money to reinvest. Long-term investors enjoy a great tax advantage. The less frequently you sell, the less Uncle Sam cuts into your future. Avoid underestimating the impact taxes can have on your holdings.

5. Buying in to the market over time has proven to be an effective strategy. Take a look at a long-term chart of the US stock markets. The gains over time are incredible. Regular investing is the key to wealth. Just keep regularly investing each month. These consistent deposits will also allow you to take advantage of market ups and downs, potentially lowering your cost basis. This is known as dollar cost averaging.

Attempting to time the market is a mistake. Short-term investing strategies create too many missed opportunities and incur too many costs, including taxes. Avoid the temptation to get in and out of the market over the short term. One of the worst mistakes you can make is making a buying or selling decision based on what you think is going to happen or how you feel. These emotional decisions could prove to be disastrous for a well-designed, diversified portfolio. It's exciting to attempt to time the market, but remember the impact of missing out on just a couple of high-return days.

FINANCIAL BELIEFS WORKSHEET

Your beliefs about money can have a negative impact on your financial situation. Recognizing and changing these beliefs can enhance your finances.

Answer these questions to gain a better perspective of how your beliefs about money might be affecting your financial circumstances, then make a plan for positive changes.

1. What part of your financial life is creating the greatest challenges?

_____

_____

_____

_____

_____

2. What are your beliefs surrounding this financial challenge?

_____

_____

_____

_____

3. Which beliefs are having the greatest negative impact?

_____

_____

_____

4. Where did this belief come from? What is it costing you?

_____

_____

_____

5. What is a more appropriate belief that will better support your financial goals?

_____

_____

_____

6. What impact would this new belief have on your finances?

_____

_____

_____

_____

7. What techniques will you use to help you adopt more financially beneficial beliefs?

_____

_____

_____

_____

8. How will you know when your beliefs have changed? What behavioral changes would you expect to see?

_____

_____

_____

_____

BUYING PRODUCTS VS. IMPLEMENTING STRATEGIES

Any decent salesperson can learn to sell financial products, and I'm sure you have purchased your share of financial products throughout the years. When you purchased or leased a vehicle, you bought auto insurance, and for a home, renters or homeowners insurance, etc. We make these purchases because they are requirements. While these must-have products are beneficial, were they purchased in the most efficient manner? You may not realize the importance of making sure every financial product you own is properly coordinated with one another. If a proper implementation strategy is not in place, it can cause substantial inefficiencies.

Perhaps you purchased your car and decided to utilize insurance company A to insure your vehicle. Then, you rent or purchase a home and insure the property with company B. It's possible you are not receiving the best rates on either. The reason for this is something called a multiline discount. Insurance companies will provide you financial incentives for using them for all lines of your property and casualty insurance.

If you have a retirement plan through your job or have a traditional IRA or Roth, you probably chose a beneficiary in the event of your death. Are you aware that a beneficiary designation will supersede a will? For example, you name your spouse as a beneficiary of your 401(k) at work and years later you get divorced. Suddenly, you pass away and had forgotten to change your beneficiary designation—your ex-spouse may have claim to that money!

Our lives are dynamic and constantly changing. When implementing financial strategies using products, flexibility is of the utmost importance. You need to be able to assess your financial situation at least once a year and know whether you are staying the course or need to pivot. Life-changing events such as marriage, birth of a child, death, disability, loss of work, or an inheritance are just some examples of when your plan should be reexamined. Too often people do planning based on what they think they need at any given time in their life. The problem is, we never know what we are going to "need" in the future. If someone told you fifteen years ago you were going to need a portable device that acts as a telephone, web browser, portable computer, etc., and if you left it at home your day would be ruined, you might think they were crazy. Nowadays, we cannot survive without our smartphones, yet we need to factor in $100 or more per month to fulfill this current everyday need. Planning should revolve around goals, not what you think you need or may need. Consistent monitoring of *all* your financial decisions is prudent.

It would be almost impossible to provide you an education on the thousands of financial products that exist today. There are products that no longer exist and those that have yet to be developed. What is important is your basic understanding of the most common products and how they may be implemented within your personal plan. It is important to note once again how each person's specific situation is different. This information should be used to enhance your understanding so you can make better informed decisions.

THE PROTECTION COMPONENT

Health insurance: Choosing options you can afford

While some people are predisposed to illness, and others like to protect themselves from the unknown, having health insurance that you can fall back on in both cases is absolutely important. The biggest challenge that many people face as it relates to health insurance is the cost.

Many businesses offer insurance plans for employees and family members. However, you may feel the need to get personal insurance of your own, or be forced to do so because your employer doesn't provide it. This is also true if you are self-employed.

How do you choose which plan might be best for you? Two main things to consider are what you can afford to pay in monthly premiums and what, if any, deductibles you may have to cover. Deductibles refer to the amounts that are required as up-front payment by the insurance company prior to them paying out claims.

Plans that offer higher monthly premiums usually cater to people who have consistent monthly financial responsibility. For example, if you're married with children and you've been employed in the same job for a number of years, a plan that offers higher monthly premiums and lower deductibles could work. This would limit the challenge of paying a lump sum payment in the event of illness.

A high-deductible plan is ideal for people who may not have the monthly income to support higher monthly premiums. If you are healthy and rarely visit a doctor, this could be a viable option. These plans usually will provide free preventive care. Keeping an emergency fund to pay expenses until you meet your deductible is wise.

Some plans may have coinsurance, which means the insurance company shares in the cost. For example, the insurance company would cover 80 percent of the expenses and you would be responsible for 20 percent. This coinsurance can be found on both high-deductible and regular health insurance plans, and should be considered.

The internet provides many websites that you can visit to compare the services of different insurance companies. In addition, under the Affordable Care Act, most states will offer subsidies for those having a lower income. You can check your state's health plan marketplace for more information. Once you're able to see plans side by side, you'll be able to determine which plan you can afford based upon the plan details. You should also contact the doctors you most frequent to see if they accept the plan before you decide to purchase it.

Health insurance is essential, and if you spend enough time looking at the options you will find a plan that is not only right for you but also for your pocket.

Expanding on health insurance – FSA, HSA, HRA, and MSA: Understanding medical expense accounts

Medical expense accounts offer a tax-advantaged means to save and pay for medical expenses that aren't commonly covered by health insurance.

The four types of accounts are:

- Flexible Spending Arrangement (FSA)
- Health Savings Account (HSA)
- Health Reimbursement Arrangement (HRA)
- Medical Savings Account (MSA)

These four accounts have different eligibility requirements and contribution rules. The benefits they give to the account holder also differ. The four types of accounts are similar, yet different:

1. Flexible Spending Arrangement. A health care FSA is a benefit provided by employers that allows an employee to set aside pre-tax funds to pay for medical expenses not covered by insurance.

- Eligibility: In general, any employee is eligible if the employer offers the program. There are exceptions if the employee is highly compensated.

- Taxes: Contributions are pre-tax.

- Contributions and distributions: Contributions are made in equal amounts over the course of the year. There is not a government-set limit to the amount of the contributions, but your employer is required to set a limit. You can use the funds for costs covered by the plan. You lose whatever money you don't spend at the end of each year.

2. Health Savings Account. This is a tax-exempt account that permits you to use your employer's contributions and earnings to pay for medical expenses.

- Eligibility: There are many requirements to set up an HSA. First, you must be covered by a qualified high deductible health plan (HDHP). You cannot be covered by any other insurance that helps with medical expenses, and you must be under sixty-five years of age and not claimed as a dependent by another person.

- Taxes: You can make pre-tax contributions to your account. You can also make post-tax deductions and then take a deduction on your tax form. Your contributions grow tax-free until you need them. Withdrawals are tax-free for qualified medical purposes.

- Contributions and distributions: You and/or your employer can make contributions. The maximum contribution is $3,200 for an individual and $6,450 for a family. IRS Publication 502 defines qualified medical expenses. Unqualified withdrawals are subject to taxes and a 20 percent penalty. The 20 percent penalty applies only to those under sixty-five.

- Funds can be rolled over each year. You don't lose the money.

3. Health Reimbursement Arrangement. An HRA is an account that is funded by the employer. Employees are reimbursed for medical expenses not covered under the employer-provided health plan.

- Eligibility: Any employee can participate if the employer has an HRA plan. Highly compensated employees may be limited in their contributions.

- Taxes: You are not taxed for your employer's contributions.

- Contributions and distributions: Only employers can make contributions. The funds can be used for all qualified expenses, which include health insurance premiums and long-term care insurance. Most employers allow unused funds to be carried over to the next year.

4. Medical Savings Account. This type of account is largely obsolete. It is very similar to the HSA, but considerably more flexible.

- Eligibility: The MSA was created for those who are self-employed and employees of small businesses.

- Taxes: The same tax benefits are found in the HSA.

- Contributions and distributions: It is not possible to start a new MSA or to contribute further to one that is already established. It is, however, permissible to maintain an existing MSA and take qualified distributions. Any unqualified withdrawals are subject to taxes and a 15 percent penalty for those under sixty-five.

- An MSA can be rolled over into an HSA.

Taking full advantage of your medical expense account can save you a lot of money! These are just the highlights of each type of medical expense account. Be sure to learn more about the type of account that may apply to your situation.

IRS Publication 969 covers all the details. Your employer's human resources department should also be able to provide further information for your unique circumstances and enable you to enjoy the maximum benefits.

Auto insurance – Most of us don't check our rates

How often do you think about your auto insurance rates? If you're like many, you don't do it too often. You may be surprised to learn that auto insurance companies periodically raise insurance rates across the board. Therefore, you might have taken the best deal for insurance when you first bound your coverage, but now you could be paying more than necessary for the same auto coverage you've had for years. That's why it's a good idea to check auto insurance rates at least yearly. This will ensure you are getting the best rates for the coverage you have. That said, as your life changes, it may be time to increase or decrease certain aspects of your coverage.

Situations that could affect your rates:

1. **Accidents.** If someone on your policy recently had an accident, your auto insurance company probably increased your rates. Interestingly, it may be possible for another insurance company to offer you lower rates despite your accident. Therefore, if you or someone in your family recently had an auto accident, it's smart to check insurance rates with other companies in order to keep your premiums low.

2. **Buying or leasing a new car.** When you're purchasing or leasing a new car, examine auto insurance rates at various companies. You should start looking at rates early in the shopping process to compare them based

on the different makes and models of cars or trucks you're considering. If not, you might make the mistake of buying a car that's quite expensive to insure.

3. **Is your teenager almost ready to drive?** If so, it's time to explore insurance coverage rates. Some auto insurance companies offer very reasonable rates for teen drivers, while others are downright exorbitant. A few months before your teenager will be driving, investigate pricing on auto insurance from companies you believe are reputable and dependable.

4. **Driving your car more or less than before.** In the event you change the number of miles you're driving each year, take the opportunity to check the rates. Although your current company might be willing to cut your rates, you should still shop the coverage with other carriers.

5. **Your car's value decreases.** As your car ages, it's wise to adjust the coverage on the car, which will reduce the amount of your premium. Although you might have full coverage on a new car, after a car is several years old, you may look to reduce certain aspects of the coverage, thus decreasing the premiums.

6. **Increase your deductible.** Even the smallest of dings, scratches, and car parts cost a pretty penny these days. Many insureds carry a $500 deductible, so in the event of needing repairs, their out-of-pocket cost

is negligible. Considering expensive parts and if in need of a minor repair for $1,500 for example, would you put in an insurance claim? More than likely your answer is no because you wouldn't want the potential of your premiums to increase. For this reason, you may want to choose a $1,000 deductible. This will save you money on your premiums, that could be earmarked for something more worthwhile.

You may be able to save hundreds of dollars yearly by comparing auto insurance companies. Make it a point to explore rates of various companies and compare them with the rates you're paying currently. And do not forget about the multiline discount by bundling the auto and home together. The savings you find with multiline discounts is better suited for your pocket than that of the insurance company.

Homeowners insurance – Ins and outs

Before you shop for homeowners insurance, it's smart to be informed about the wide range of policy costs and declarations of insuring your home. Learning as much as you can about the following will help you select the best homeowners insurance to meet your goals. This education should help you make the right choices on choosing the best policy.

1. **Home type.** Your homeowners insurance policy should reflect the type of home you have. Policies vary,

depending on whether you live in a condominium, co-op, or house.

Typical insurance coverage. A basic homeowners insurance policy will cover damage to your home from many perils such as fire, vandalism, and weather events. There are exceptions for items such as earthquakes and floods, and coverage can be attained by purchasing a separate policy. Other "structures" that are built on your property, such as garages, toolsheds, or workshops are usually included in homeowners insurance. Another important inclusion in a typical policy is personal liability. This coverage protects you if someone gets hurt on your property.

2.   **Home construction.** What is your home made of? Is it built sturdily to handle weather events?

   •   Materials used in the construction of your home will partially determine the type of insurance you obtain as well as the cost.

   •   The more superior the construction, the easier it will be for you to find a good policy.

3.   **Quality home care.** If you go the extra mile to protect your home and belongings, you might attain a reduced premium. For example, if you live in a hurricane zone and install hurricane shutters on all your doors and

windows, you might score a reduced rate on your basic insurance policy.

4. **Deductible levels.** As with other types of insurance, you can save money on your homeowners insurance policy if you're willing to have higher deductible amounts. Be aware that your mortgage company might have specific requirements or set limits as to how high of a deductible you can have.

5. **Replacement cost coverage.** It's wise to know the value of the property you're insuring, plus an approximate value of your personal items inside the dwelling that you'll be insuring. Knowing these values will help the agent decide how much to insure your property for. To figure replacement costs, insurance companies will typically write a policy that covers 125 percent to 200 percent of the price of your property.

6. **Cost of insurance.** Many factors affect the cost of your homeowners insurance policy. Some of those factors are the age of the dwelling, the size of your home, its location, and the construction materials. Interestingly enough, your location relative to fire protection services such as a fire hydrant can have an impact.

7. **Insurance company's reputation.** As with any business you deal with, know your insurance company's reputation. Verify they are licensed to sell

insurance in your state. Check the company's ratings through Standard & Poor's, TheStreet.com, and your local Better Business Bureau.

Obtaining homeowners insurance requires you to do your homework. Once you familiarize yourself with all the facts related to your dwelling, you'll be prepared and ready to make an educated decision. You should also read the policy when you get it. Make sure it contains all the parameters you want. Don't be afraid to ask questions of your insurance agent, including the potential of a multiline discount.

Umbrella liability insurance – Why you need it

Living in a litigious society, coupled with the unimaginable situation that might happen to you financially, you should consider purchasing umbrella liability insurance. This insurance can protect your assets from large claims or lawsuits.

1. An umbrella policy is additional insurance. You can purchase an umbrella liability insurance policy as an adjunct to your homeowners or auto insurance policy. With some policies, you can also add to other coverage, like for a boat, with an additional charge.

2. These policies are designed to provide extra financial protection. Your auto and home policies have basic liability limits as a basic policy feature. If for some reason a person was injured in excess of those limits,

what would you do? This is where an umbrella policy would help.

3. Umbrella policies are large, but your assets don't have to be. The least amount of liability protection you can obtain through an umbrella policy is $1 million. Also, most umbrella liability policies require that your main policy (vehicle or homeowners insurance) cover you for at least $300,000 to $500,000. It's not necessary for you to have $1 million worth of assets in order to obtain such coverage, or to be sued for such an amount. After all, you could, for example, get sued for a million dollars and have assets totaling only $200,000. Without an umbrella policy, your future income and assets could also be at risk!

4. An umbrella policy covers everyone in your family living in your household, including your pets. Even if your pets get loose and cause damage to property or harm another animal or person, you're covered. Many policies even extend coverage to others, such as when you let someone else drive your car and they get in an accident.

5. Umbrella liability coverage may pay for your legal fees if a liability suit is brought against you.

6. The cost for umbrella insurance is reasonable. The first $1 million of coverage costs as little as $200 to $400 per year. Each additional $1 million is only about

$100. Raising your regular deductible might even provide enough savings to pay for an extra million dollars of coverage! This is where the coordination and implementation of insurance strategies are crucial.

7.   Ask your auto or home insurance agent about adding an umbrella liability policy to your coverage. You might get discounts on all your liability policies when you bundle all of them with the same carrier. Once again, the multiline discount!

Life insurance – What the average agent won't explain to you

Life insurance can be complicated, and most of us know we need it, but we don't really know what kind to get, how much we should get, when we should get it, if it should be owned in a trust or not, and how long we should keep it.

A life insurance policy should provide you with peace of mind in the event of your untimely death. With some types of life insurance, you also have the option to access a cash "bucket" of money for emergencies, to supplement your retirement income, or to help create added flexibility for things such as maximizing a pension.

Before addressing any of the above questions, first you need to understand how insurance companies calculate premiums. Your age, health, family medical history, occupation, hobbies, whether you smoke, prescriptions, and motor vehicle records are just some of what insurance companies look at. These are called mortality expenses. They will also consider general expenses the insurance company will endure to operate, such as commissions to agents, payroll, and any other costs associated with running the company.

It is always advised that you compare rates among insurance companies, but you must be sure the parameters to create the quotes are identical. For example, if you are a forty-five-year-old nonsmoker, but you take medication for high blood pressure and high cholesterol, more than likely you will not be entitled to the best rates (elite or ultra-preferred). Should you receive quotes from two different agents, but one provided a quote based on the best rate and the other was more realistic and provided rates at the second tier (preferred), you may be more inclined to work with the first agent.

What you need to know is, the rates are the rates, no matter what agent you choose. While premiums can change between carriers, they cannot differ if all the parameters are equal with the same carrier. Rates are regulated by the individual states.

What if you are offered life insurance through your employer? It's important you understand the pros and cons. The benefit of purchasing life insurance through your employer is that you more than likely won't have to take a medical exam. This is extremely beneficial if you have a medical condition. In addition, the premiums are extremely inexpensive and usually taken from your paycheck. When this happens, you certainly don't "feel" the payment each month. While this is attractive, the downside is coverage is often limited. Typically, the insurance company will cover you only for a multiple of salary. Depending upon how much you make, this will more than likely not be enough to keep your family from having to go live on the in-laws' couch! In addition, if you leave your job for any reason, you probably leave your life insurance too. You may not be so lucky with your next employer's benefits package, and it will be on you to buy life insurance on your own. The moral of the story here is to consider the employer-offered life insurance a "bonus." It's worth paying for it to have a little extra coverage.

An aside: there are some insurance agents that represent only one insurance company. These are called "captive agents." Insurance companies underwriting guidelines are all different. For example, one insurance company may be more lenient than another when it comes to the body mass index (BMI). If you choose to use a captive agent, and the company they represent doesn't have a favorable BMI index, you may be forced into paying that higher premium. You should always ask the insurance agent if they can provide you quotes from multiple insurance companies. If they can't, do your due diligence in finding a true independent agent. This philosophy can also be applied to your auto and homeowners insurance too.

Types of Life Insurance

There are many variations of the most common types of life insurance, but to make it simple, the designs mentioned below are the most common. In addition, these policies can offer riders (additional features) that could provide added benefits. With these added benefits will come additional costs. For example, the most common rider is something known as waiver of premium. This means if you were to be declared disabled by a medical professional, the insurance company would not require you pay your premiums anymore. Hence, they are waived, and your policy remains in force.

Term insurance is the simplest and most affordable option. The length of time (term) varies but is usually between five and thirty years. When you think of term insurance, think of the word "terminates" in your mind. Once the length of time has been reached, the policy will terminate. Both the premiums and the death benefit will stay the same over the term period chosen. Term is useful for people who have children, mortgages, and various liabilities. The appropriate amount of protection can cover these expenses and more. One thing to keep in mind is if you still desire coverage after a term policy's period ends, factors such as poor health and age will result in higher premiums when you buy a new policy. Therefore, it is best that you buy as much as you can when you are young and healthy.

Whole life insurance, also known as "cash value" or "ordinary life" insurance, is a consistent type of "permanent" life insurance that remains in effect your entire life at a level premium. While premiums are significantly higher than term insurance, a portion of your premium goes into a reserve fund called "cash value" that increases each year the policy is in effect. The cash value will grow tax-deferred, and you can withdraw and/or borrow those funds. (In the event of death, the death benefit will be reduced by the amount withdrawn or borrowed.) Depending on the insurance company you purchase this type of policy from, you could also be entitled to dividends that may be put toward the cash value and an increasing death benefit.

The premiums must generally remain constant over the life of the policy and must be paid periodically according to the amount indicated in the policy. That said, there may be a point in time when dividends and/or cash value are high enough to pay the premiums on your behalf. This could be useful later in the policy years and during retirement because you would no longer have the outlay from your cash flow to continue paying the premiums.

While term insurance is a true cost to you, (unrecoverable expense), whole life is an outlay (recoverable, i.e., cash value, death benefit). Whole life is probably not for most people, but for those who can afford the outlay, there could be tremendous benefit. Whole life insurance is most suitable for you, if you want to:

- Use it as a tax and estate-planning vehicle.

- Accumulate cash value for a child's education or your retirement.

- Pay final expenses (funeral).

- Provide money for a favorite charity.

- Fund a business buy/sell agreement.

- Provide a key businessperson protection.

- Maximize a spouse's pension.

- Create a tax-efficient family legacy.

Whole life insurance cash value returns will typically fluctuate with the interest rate environment; however, most insurance companies will offer a guaranteed growth rate. It is important to understand that cash value will not usually follow returns available from other investments like equity mutual funds.

Before buying whole life, you need to think carefully about choosing your level of coverage. Too often people make the mistake of wanting all the benefits it has to offer, and the death benefit they purchase is insufficient. Even worse, they financially overextend themselves, making it difficult to sustain paying such high premiums. This would be a tragic error because defaulting on premium payments can mean policy cancellation, loss of premiums paid, loss of cash value, and potentially taxes owed. You must be careful and work with a professional who really understands your situation and the inner workings of how these policies are designed. You should:

- Pick a life insurance policy that has a guaranteed cash value starting within the first couple of years.

- Consider "participating" insurance policies (usually mutual companies) that can pay dividends, increasing your policy's value by boosting both the total cash value and the death benefits.

- Beware of any insurance policy that levies "surrender charges" if you cancel.

- Find out if the policy offers an automatic premium loan. Meaning, if you ever need to stop paying premiums, your policy allows for the use of the accumulated cash value of the life insurance policy to pay the premiums, thus keeping your coverage current.

Universal life. Like whole life insurance, you have the potential to build cash value with this type of policy. These policies are known for their flexibility because they allow you to vary your life insurance premium payments. That said, you must be extremely careful when implementing this type of strategy.

Unlike whole life and term insurance, mortality and expense charges (M&E) are calculated on an annual basis. Both term and whole life insurance premiums are "level," meaning, they don't change. The insurance company has already factored in the M&E when the premium amount in provided. Many universal life quotes look much more attractive than whole life because the premiums illustrated could be significantly less. The key here is the premiums quoted are usually what's called a "target" premium. This target premium is a suggested minimum amount that should be paid to keep the death benefit in force for your entire life, hopefully! You may be wondering why I used the word "hopefully" if universal life is considered permanent insurance.

Here's the reason. Think of universal life as a funnel, but with a cap on the bottom. The insurance company will calculate the mortality and expense charges each year that will go toward paying your premium. The balance will be placed into the funnel to earn interest, or to be invested in mutual funds (variable universal life) or a stock market index (index universal life). The concept is that each year the cash value should grow at a projected rate of return. The cash value could then be used to withdraw or borrow against similar to that of whole life.

Here's where the problem lies. Each year, you get older and the M&E charges increase. It will take some time, but eventually the amount of premium needed to cover these charges may be more than the target premium the insurance company originally factored. At this time, the cap is removed from the bottom of the funnel, and the insurance company will use your cash value to cover the premium shortfall! Once the funnel is empty, the policy will lapse with no death benefit or cash value. This could be a major disruption in your plan if your intent was to have life-long death benefit protection.

The key to making this type of plan successful is to pay more than the target premium each year. This will help to maintain the longevity of the policy. You also need to closely manage the underlying investments the cash value is linked to. It is recommended you look at this each year with your advisor so you can strategize on how much to be paying toward premiums.

Standard no-cash-value life insurance policies like term life insurance invest life insurance premiums in ultralow-risk funds that are often obliged to return a certain level of interest. This provides the insurance company with confidence in receiving a tangible level of return, which is transferred through to the life insurance policyholder by way of a guaranteed lump sum payment upon death or terminal illness.

Variable and indexed life insurance is different from standard types of life insurance, as the company hands the investment reins over to the policyholder. The insurance company may allow a percentage, or in many cases all the cash value, to be invested by the policyholder. Variable and indexed life policies come with the disclaimer that the life insurance company takes no responsibility for the performance of the variable life policyholder's investments. Therefore, if the investments perform poorly, the policyholder accepts the consequences that there will be little or no cash surrender value when the insurance is redeemed. Hence, the cap being taken off the bottom of the funnel. To make matters worse, if you were withdrawing cash value simultaneous to market or interest rate declines, the funnel runs out faster. This could also cause a negative taxable event!

It is very important to think long and hard about these types of life insurance policies before opting to take one on. There is a high level of risk involved. Ideally, variable life policies should be taken out only by seasoned investors who know their way around the investment markets. If you've never invested in the stock market before and if you don't plan on paying more than the target premium, then a variable or indexed life policy is probably not for you.

Not all universal life policies were created equal! There is a product called guaranteed universal life. It is exactly as the name suggests: guaranteed for life. Think of this type of policy as permanent term insurance. While there may be a few years of cash value shown on an illustration, it is not designed for the cash value to ever be used. These policies are often used in estate-planning situations where cash value is not necessary, but a permanent death benefit is needed. The premiums are often less than that of whole life because of the absence of cash value. You can specify a specific number of years you wish to have death benefit coverage, and the premium will be calculated accordingly. The premiums and the death benefit will be level for the specific number of years you choose to illustrate.

How Much Do You Need?

One of the most important aspects of implementing a life insurance strategy is that people don't put enough consideration into how much coverage is actually enough. When looking at life quotes, how can you determine how much will actually be needed by your family if they no longer have you to depend on?

Insurance companies typically allow two methods of determining the appropriate amount of death benefit a person can bind. One is by conducting a "needs analysis," and the other is by using a formula called "human life value."

When using the needs analysis method, you should make a list including but not limited to: money spent on daily expenses, elderly family care, childcare, education, food, clothing, mortgage, car or other vehicle payments, and various forms of debt including loans and credit cards. Then you should consider the costs for your final expenses, such as your funeral, burial, and any other necessary medical or hospital costs. Also included in the needs analysis should be potential future expenses and savings. This should include college tuition and a retirement fund for your spouse. If you want to leave any funds to charities or organizations, you can factor that in as well.

Once you have completed the needs analysis, you may choose to subtract your current assets. While some will do this, others choose to exclude them. This is completely a personal preference.

On September 11, 2001, when the World Trade Center was attacked, the Widows and Orphans Fund was used to compensate victims. There was quite a bit of uproar as to the amounts that were distributed to each of the victims. Why did some receive significantly more than others? The reason for this is called human life value. It's certainly difficult to place a monetary value on a human life, but for situations like the above, or to purchase life insurance, it's necessary.

The formula to calculate human life value is the present value of future earnings. For example, if you are forty years old and make $200,000 per year, your human life value would be $5 million. This considers the salary earned for the next twenty-five years. If this person were to die and the death benefit received, a 5 percent distribution rate at a 0 percent rate of return would provide for $250,000 of income replacement each year for those twenty-five years, therefore, replacing the loss of income to their family.

Now that you have a good idea of how much you are going to need, you can now start to receive quotes. Remember to always compare companies using the same parameters. It is extremely important that you do your homework. Make sure you don't purchase too little coverage. Doing a thorough needs analysis or using your human life value will ensure that your family is safe and protected even if you pass away unexpectedly.

When Should I Get Life Insurance?

Most people do understand the purpose of life insurance and why it's important even if they choose not to purchase it. There are many reasons to purchase insurance, and they are usually identified by "life-changing events"—for example, the birth of child, debt obligations, divorce, or you own a business.

The moment you are responsible for another person in your life, you need life insurance. If someone counts on your ability to earn an income, then life insurance is a necessity. If you have a mortgage, you need life insurance to pay off the remainder of the mortgage or other debts, your heirs shouldn't have to be responsible to deal with the debt. If you own a business, are partners in a business, or are a key employee in a business, a life insurance policy can keep that business afloat.

While people often associate life insurance with a life changing event, some can make the argument it's never too early to buy life insurance. This includes a newborn child! After all, the younger you are, usually the healthier you are.

Many people argue that children do not need life insurance. Insurance is typically used for individuals who have something to lose in the event of their untimely death. Adults often provide for their family, while children are beloved and indispensable on an emotional and mental level. Children very rarely offer their family any financial or monetary stability. As such, it is unlikely that from a financial standpoint individuals would have something to lose from the death of a child.

On the other side of the argument, some people feel insuring a child is a good strategy to implement for many reasons. As a person gets older, their life insurance premiums will almost always increase over time. This is because people often subject themselves to short-term or long-term life-threatening practices, such as smoking, drinking, not eating healthy, driving vehicles including motorcycles, and the like. Children, on the other hand, are innocent and limited in their exposure. Children can get some of the lowest insurance premiums offered by life insurance companies.

Not only is insurability a factor, but the potential for multigenerational wealth building is phenomenal. Nobody purchases a life insurance policy with the assumption the child will die, but rather for the multigenerational benefit it provides.

Typically, a child is insured using a whole life policy. While the child is young, a parent would be a beneficiary in case of the worst happening, but eventually when the child has their own family, this would change, naming their children as beneficiaries. If the plan is designed correctly, the cash value could be accessed if needed any time during the child's life, and at their life expectancy the death benefit would pass to the next generation. There are very few ways to pass wealth in a tax-efficient manner between generations, and this is certainly one way to do it. Keep in mind, while this strategy is great, it's important to work with an advisor who can lay out the details. For example, policy ownership, amount, type of insurance, affordability, etc.

Should It be Owned in Trust or Not?

One tool that is commonly used by those with considerable wealth to deal with estate/inheritance taxes is life insurance, more specifically, owned by an irrevocable life insurance trust (ILIT).

There are many benefits to this type of trust:

- It provides tremendous flexibility. Wealthy individuals do not always have wealthy heirs. Handling paying for estate taxes, which can be as high as 40 percent, can be terribly burdensome for many. Your heirs may be forced to sell real estate, stocks, bonds, or even personal property to raise the necessary cash.

- When set up properly, the assets owned by the ILIT aren't considered part of the estate. In a nutshell, your heirs don't have to pay taxes on any assets within the trust.

- The death benefit is also excluded from estate taxes. Therefore, in nearly all cases, life insurance proceeds paid to the ILIT would be exempt from taxes and can be used to pay any estate taxes that may come due.

For smaller estates, even if taxes aren't a critical issue, life insurance owned in a trust can provide great flexibility and peace of mind for all involved. For example, when a spouse is not good at managing money, a large windfall intended for specific uses may wind up being spent elsewhere.

While life insurance can be a great estate-planning tool, keep in mind that trusts can be complicated, and it's important to find an attorney with the knowledge and experience to set it up properly.

Disability Insurance – Your Most Valuable Asset Is You

Most of us have insured our house, possessions, cars, and our lives. However, have you insured something that might be even more important: your ability to consistently earn income. This may be the most important asset you have.

Consider the following: if you currently earn $50,000 a year and you're thirty-five years old, from now until you're sixty-five you'll earn $1.5 million. That assumes your income never increases, which it almost certainly will.

Doesn't that seem like it might be worth protecting? Is your house or car worth $1.5 million? Most of us don't own any single object worth $1.5 million.

Disability insurance insures your ability to earn income. Many people hear the word "disability" and immediately think of an accident. But most long-term disabilities are the result of illness, such as heart disease or cancer. Every year, over 12 percent of adults in the United States have a long-term disability.

Not only that, but one out of seven employed residents of the United States will have a disability that lasts five years or longer before age sixty-five. The odds of suffering a disability that lasts at least three months is over 50 percent. The US Department of Housing and Urban Development has estimated that 45 percent of foreclosures are due to disability.

You may be thinking Social Security or workers' compensation will help. While Social Security might provide some benefit, these two forms of income are rather limited, even for the most frugal of people. In addition, qualifying is not always easy. If you're injured at your place of employment and unable to work, you're covered under workers' compensation. However, you're three times more likely to receive an injury outside of work that limits your ability to work. You don't receive workers' compensation if that happens.

Large employers typically offer short-term and long-term disability insurance. This coverage is frequently affordable and will cover 50 percent to 60 percent of your salary. The total payout may also be capped, and the benefit is usually paid as taxable income. Using the same example above, if you make $50,000 per year and are covered for 60 percent of your salary at work, your benefit would be $30,000. Once you pay tax on that, there won't be much left. Similar to group life insurance, if this is offered through your employer, take it, and consider it bonus coverage.

It is recommended you purchase your own disability policy outside of your employer. Depending on the factors, they could be expensive but have far more flexibility to provide what you need. The cost of an individual policy can vary dramatically. You could expect to pay 1 percent to 3 percent of your salary annually to replace 60 percent of your salary. In addition, these policy benefits are typically paid to you tax free.

Some factors that influence the premium include:

1. **The monthly payout.** Obviously, the more money you would receive in the event you suffer a disability, the more your policy will cost.

2. **How "disability" is defined.** Does it pay if you are unable to do your job? Or does it pay only if you are unable to do your job and any other job for which you're qualified? What if you can work part of a day, but not the whole day? Be sure you know what you're getting, and what you're not getting.

3. **How long is the waiting period before you start receiving your payments?** The longer the waiting period, the less expensive the policy will be. This is a good reason to have that three-to-six-month cash reserve you're always hearing about. If you don't currently have it set aside, get started today.

4. **Your occupation.** Some jobs are simply more hazardous than others. Everything else being equal, a

construction worker should expect to pay more than an accountant.

5. **Cost of living.** Some policies cover cost of living increases. This can make a big difference, depending on the length of your disability.

6. **Additional purchase option.** Once you're insured, this option would allow you to purchase additional coverage later on without having to submit to another physical.

Disability insurance is the insurance that everyone seems to forget about, especially those who are self-employed. But this may be the most important insurance you can purchase! Look into disability insurance today; your future and the future of your family may depend on it.

Long-Term Care Insurance – Also Known as Inheritance Insurance

One of the largest medical costs you're likely to incur in your lifetime is long-term care. Long-term care means that you require care by a skilled medical professional to be provided either in your home or in an assisted living or nursing facility because you can't fulfill basic activities of daily living. Most long-term care policies will pay a benefit if two of six activities cannot be met. They are: eating, bathing, dressing, mobility, continence, and toileting. This type of care is very expensive.

For care outside of the home, a private room in a nursing home can cost over $75,000 a year. Long-term care insurance, while not cheap, can reduce that burden.

As with everything else, this type of insurance has its benefits and drawbacks. Have you considered long-term care insurance in your retirement planning? Imagine you saved for your retirement all throughout your working years, just to have to spend it on caring for yourself.

The biggest criticism of these policies has been their cost. However, this insurance can save you a tremendous amount of money in medical expenses and simultaneously preserve your assets.

When looking for a policy you have several choices:

1. **Daily benefit amount.** This is the maximum amount the policy will pay per day for care. You can typically choose from $50/day to $500/day. Policies often specify a maximum monthly amount instead. This is nice because you can then opt to receive more care on some days and less on others.

2. **Different amounts in different settings.** Some policies will let you choose the different benefit amounts for different settings. Maybe you feel comfortable with $100/day at home but would rather have $150/day in a long-term care facility.

3. **Benefit period.** This is the maximum time the policy will remain in effect based on the daily or monthly benefit amount.

4. **Comprehensive or facility care.** Some insurance covers only care that you receive in a long-term care facility. Other policies are considered to be "comprehensive" and allow for a wider range of services. Most insurance sold today is comprehensive, but be sure to check before you sign on the dotted line. Facility care policies are available for those who feel confident that their family and friends are willing and able to care for them at home

5. **Additional benefits:** As with other types of insurance, there are many other options or "riders" that can be added to the basic coverage.

   • *Inflation protection* is a popular option. If you're unlikely to need care until far in the future, this is worth looking into. How much are health care costs going to rise in the next twenty-five years? Likely a lot. There are many types of inflation protection, so be sure of what you're actually getting.

Here are some additional costs that long-term care insurance may or may not cover. Do your research!

- Modification of your home. This would include augmentations like ramps and grab bars.

- Transportation to medical appointments.

- Training a relative or a friend to provide personal care properly.

- In-home medical equipment.

Some policies will even pay your friends or family members to provide care to you. These payouts tend to be rather small and may cover only the cost that the care provider incurs. While most policies will not provide payment under these circumstances, some offer cash payment for each day you're in the care of a non-medical professional.

Long-term care insurance is something every person should seriously consider. The cost of the policy can be high, but the cost of not having a policy can be catastrophic. Even a sixty-five-year-old millionaire can run out of money in a hurry should they require long-term care.

These policies tend to have more options and exceptions than other types of insurance, so be sure to really do your research or sit down with an independent insurance agent you trust.

BONUS MATERIAL!
HOW TO PASS YOUR INSURANCE MEDICAL EXAMS AND GET YOUR BEST RATE

Have you ever studied hard for an exam? Even though you might not have been paying close attention all semester, it can still be worthwhile to cram at the last minute. In many cases you can apply the same tactic to your insurance exams. While it's better to be healthy all the time, there are things you can do right now to improve your medical exam results.

1. **Avoid drinking alcohol for at least forty-eight hours before the appointment.** While alcohol feels relaxing, it also tends to increase blood pressure. Blood pressure that is a little high can increase your rate 20 percent. If it's too high, you can be out of luck altogether.

2. **Avoid caffeine for forty-eight hours.** Like alcohol, caffeine can raise blood pressure. It can also increase your heart rate and temporarily create an irregular heartbeat.

   • Remember that it's not just coffee that contains caffeine. Tea, soft drinks, pain relievers, and cold medications can also have caffeine. Even a small amount can have a significant effect in some people.

3. **Drop excess weight.** This tactic requires more time than the previous two, but it's important. Obesity is a risk factor for many common causes of death. Just a few pounds can potentially move you into the next rate category. Lose some weight, and save a lot of money.

4. **Stop smoking.** Interestingly, if you've smoked for the last thirty years but have stopped for about a year, you may be considered a nonsmoker. This is perhaps the most important tip. Smoking can increase your premium by 200 percent. That's a threefold increase. Eliminating your smoking habit can cut your premium by two thirds.

   • If you're going to continue to smoke, avoid smoking for at least an hour before the exam. Your blood pressure and pulse will be improved.

5. **Avoid the health club for twenty-four hours.** Overtraining can result in unusual blood pressure, pulse, and other blood values. Any exercise shortly before your appointment can also have negative effects. Avoid working out for twenty-four hours before, and give yourself a longer break if you've really been pushing yourself hard at the gym.

6. **Eat in a very healthy manner for at least a couple of meals leading up to the appointment.** Even one meal of fatty meat can raise lipid and cholesterol levels for a short period of time. You should also fast for twelve hours before the appointment.

   • Ideally, eat well for at least three weeks before your exam. According to research, any diet will show maximal improvement in blood results after just three weeks.

7. **Rest and relax.** A good night's sleep will lower your pulse and blood pressure.

Most of these tips require only a day or two to put into action. A few require more time but are likely to have a profound effect on the cost of your life insurance premiums.

THE ASSET ACCUMULATION COMPONENT

This part of planning is certainly more exciting than talking about death and disability. That said, before investing your money, it's imperative you have your goals and cash flow in order. Where do you see yourself in five, ten, twenty, or thirty years? Do you want to own your home free and clear? Pay for your child's college education out of pocket? Retire early through the fruits of your investments?

Once you confirm your cash flow analysis and you know where every dollar is allocated, you can then focus on how and where to allot the excess positive cash flow. Clearly, the more money you're able to put into your investments, the more likely you are to achieve your goals. In the realm of investments, the adage is true: it takes money to make money. And you have to start somewhere.

There are multiple ways you can invest your money, and it's important you have a clear understanding of what they are and how they work. Before we get into the nitty-gritty, it's pertinent you understand some basic terms.

Financial terms can be intimidating. The financial industry can even seem to have its own language that can be confusing to the average investor. However, if you understand the terminology, you'll gain the confidence you need to make positive, informed decisions.

Below you'll find some of the most common financial terms and acronyms used in the world of banking, investment, and real estate. While trying to make sense of all these terms could be overwhelming, it's really not that difficult.

To prove this, let's talk about sunglasses and umbrellas! Let's pretend you are going to open a store on the beach. First, you need to figure out what you are going to sell in your store. One item that may be attractive is sunglasses. Do you think you should offer only one brand, like Ray-Ban, or do you want to sell multiple brands, and why? If you sell only one brand, you run into an issue of them being too expensive for some people, or others may want to spend more money. Perhaps you have customers that don't like the way Ray-Bans look and want a larger selection. In order for your store to be profitable, you should stock it with several brands so you have a diversified inventory.

To take this a step further, what if it rains? And for the purpose of this explanation, we will assume our customers may choose to go to the beach when it rains! In this case, we also want to make sure we have umbrellas in stock in case of a rainy day. Once again, this creates further diversification in your store. You now will be fully prepared with inventory that can be sold in different weather conditions and you have variety (diversification).

If you have ever walked the streets of a major city when it's raining outside and are unfortunate enough to have left your umbrella at home, you may not have to search too far to purchase one. When it rains, you may find street vendors on the corner offering to sell you the umbrella you so desperately need. The issue you may potentially face is the umbrella you are about to purchase is more expensive on the day it's raining. This is an instant example of supply and demand. On a bright and sunny day, you probably could've purchased that same umbrella for less money. Because it's raining and you need it right now, you are willing to pay a premium, and the seller knows it.

You may have heard something like this, "You want to buy into the market when it's low and sell when it's high." While this is great in theory, it is difficult to accomplish this. Nobody has a crystal ball, just like weather is also predicted. If you don't know when it's going to be sunny and when it's going to rain, you just need to make sure your store is always properly stocked and with the right merchandise.

Let's look at the most common types of investments that exist. This will be the merchandise we will use to stock our store. There are many types of investments to choose from, and each come with some level of risk. It is crucial to identify your own personal risk limitations when choosing investments. As a general concept, you'll be able to choose from low-risk, low-yield investments or high-risk, high-yield investments. When you see the term "yield" as mentioned above, it usually corresponds to purchasing bonds. Below, we'll identify just how risky some of the most popular types of investments can be and what the investments themselves entail.

Stocks: When you purchase a stock, you're purchasing a small portion of the corporation by becoming a shareholder. Companies issue shares of stock as a method to raise money. Stocks are considered riskier investments because the market is unpredictable. What you need to consider is while stocks are considered more volatile, the risk versus reward is much greater. As an owner of the company, you, in essence, participate in the profit and losses. If the company you invest in goes bankrupt, you can lose your entire investment; however, if the company is profitable, you could have unlimited growth potential.

Bonds: Purchasing bonds makes you a creditor of a company, rather than a shareholder. Issuing bonds is another method companies use to raise capital, just differently. As a creditor, you're loaning your money for a specified amount of time. In exchange for your loan, the company will pay you the principal amount in addition to interest. This promise to pay, along with the interest you earn, is why bonds are considered safer investments than stocks. Just remember, a company who issues bonds still can go bankrupt, but in this case, you become a creditor.

Even if you never received your investment (loan) back, you more than likely would've received something in return in the form of the interest you were paid.

CDs: When you invest in a certificate of deposit, you're agreeing to loan the CD issuer (usually the bank) your money for a specific amount of time. You're able to remove your funds at your discretion. By removing the funds before the agreed upon date (the maturity date), you'll incur a fee. CDs are very low-risk investments; however, this low risk also leads to a low return.

Mutual funds: Mutual funds are appealing to investors because they offer a diversified portfolio of stocks, bonds, and other types of investments all wrapped into one. Rather than investing privately, a mutual fund collects money from multiple private investors and uses the money to invest in several diversified investments. Investors then receive shares of the investments and are free to hold or sell them at their discretion. They trade only once a day, and the price is calculated after the stock market closes. Mutual funds are a great way to diversify because instead of only owning one stock or bond, you can own several at one time. Mutual funds can be actively managed, where the manager creates a mix of investments to meet the fund's stated objective. They can also be passively managed, in which case the fund manager attempts to track the performance of a particular index.

ETFs: Exchange-traded funds (ETFs) have been available since 1993. They have grown in popularity every year since their inception. A simple way to view ETFs is to consider them like mutual funds that trade like stocks. They are traded throughout the day, and price will fluctuate based on supply and demand. Mutual fund shares are always purchased and sold directly. The tax advantages are one of the most significant advantages of ETFs.

While the above-mentioned are the most common types of investments, it's important to understand the terms and concepts that go along with them. Many of the below are definitions, but you don't want to miss out on some valuable planning concepts found within. Knowledge is power and will help you to make smart decisions.

The Broad Stock Market

Annual report: All publicly traded companies are required by the Securities and Exchange Commission to produce an annual report. The report is sent to all shareholders and provides the financial results for the previous fiscal year. Accredited accounting firms review and verify the results.

Balance sheet: This is a full accounting of a company's assets, liabilities, equity, and net worth at a certain point in time. A balance sheet is included as part of the annual report and effectively tells you what the company is worth.

Bear market: A bear market is one where there are considerable and long-term declines in the value of the market, typically for two or more quarters. There is not a precise or agreed-upon definition for this common term.

Blue chip: The most stable and prestigious stocks on the stock market. Companies like General Electric and IBM are frequently considered to be blue chip stocks.

Bull market: The opposite of a bear market is a bull market. Two quarters of significant stock market growth and a positive outlook are characteristics of a bull market. This also usually means that there are more buyers than sellers, which drives up prices.

Capital gain: Assets that are held for less than one year and sold for a profit are subject to ordinary income tax. This is also called a short-term capital gain. An asset that is held for more than one year and sold for a profit is considered a long-term capital gain and taxed at a lower rate. The tax laws constantly change as will your personal ordinary income tax rate, so it's important to know your personal tax circumstances. This will allow you to make intelligent decisions when you are buying and selling.

Common stock: The basic unit of ownership in a corporation. Holders of common stock have certain rights, including voting on major issues concerning the corporation. When you buy stock, you are usually buying common stock.

Diversification: Investing broadly across a number of different securities, industries, or asset classes to reduce risk. This is a principal advantage of investing in mutual funds.

Dividends: Profits paid to shareholders of the company. The board of directors authorizes the payment, usually quarterly. Commonly, dividends are in the form of cash, but may instead be additional shares of stock. Dividends are taxable. Companies with good opportunities for growth will usually elect to spend the money on expansion rather than giving it back to the shareholders in dividends, theoretically resulting in higher prices for the stock, which means greater gains for shareholders when they sell their stock.

Dollar-cost averaging: The practice of investing a fixed amount of money on a regular basis. This strategy results in buying more shares of an investment when the price is lower, and buying fewer shares when the price is higher, which lowers the average price paid for the shares. Also, this popular investment strategy promotes regular and consistent investing.

EPS or earnings per share: This is calculated by dividing a company's net revenue by the number of outstanding shares. This number is commonly used to compare different companies on a per-share basis.

The Fed or Federal Reserve Board: This organization ultimately controls the nation's interest rates. Consequently, the Fed has a tremendous influence on the stock market.

Fundamental analysis: This method for analyzing a stock looks at basic key ratios and attempts to understand the underlying business. This is normally undertaken to determine if additional analysis is worthwhile.

Growth stocks: These stocks usually don't pay a dividend but instead choose to put profits back into the company to finance additional growth. Investors buy growth stock for its potential price appreciation as the company grows.

Hedge fund: A private investment pool for qualified investors. Hedge funds are exempt from SEC registration. Among the various qualifications is a significant amount of wealth; the minimum investment is typically $1 million or more. The risk and rewards can both be very high for hedge funds.

Income statements: Financial documents listing the income and expenses of a company.

Index: An index is comprised of a hypothetical portfolio made up of securities (stocks, bonds, etc.) that tracks the broader markets or a market sector (real estate, technology, etc.). It is often used by investors as a benchmark to evaluate the performance of their portfolio. Each individual security can be associated with an underlying index.

Index fund: A fund intended to mimic the performance of a market index. In essence, it's like owning a share of the entire market within that stock, bond, or sector index.

Inflation: This occurs when the money supply is too great. It is a rise in price of a specific "bucket" of consumer goods. The percent increase from the last measurement is called the inflation rate. Interest rates will tend to rise overall, and this will slow market growth. Inflation has a direct effect on a portfolio and is a risk you must consider. For example, if you have a portfolio that returned 8 percent and inflation is at 3 percent, you really earned only 5 percent.

IPO or initial public offering: The initial offering of a company's stock. Also used in mutual funds terminology, an IPO is a closed-end fund's first offering of shares in that fund.

Joint tenants with rights of survivorship (JTWROS): This is the way most accounts are titled when a joint account is opened between spouses. While its use isn't limited to only spouses, it is most commonly used this way. A JTWROS has two equal owners, and if one person were to pass away, the other person will receive full ownership of the account. They also have equal rights to the decisions made in the account while they are both living.

Liquidity: When an investment can be quickly converted to cash, it is said to have a high amount of liquidity.

Margin: A method to finance stock purchases. The stock that you already own is used as collateral for loan. The loan is then used to purchase additional stock.

Margin call: If the stock you're using as collateral loses too much value, you must correct the situation by either depositing more money or selling other securities.

Market capitalization or market cap: A way of measuring the size of a company. A market capitalization is simply the current stock price multiplied by the number of outstanding shares. A stock trading at $75 with one hundred million outstanding shares would have a market cap of $7.5 billion.

Market order: An order to buy or sell a stock at the best available current price. A limit order specifies an exact price at which to buy or sell. A limit order may or may not be executed; a market order is executed immediately.

Mid cap: This type of stock is any company with a market capitalization between $1 billion and $8 billion.

Nasdaq: This is a stock exchange of primarily technological companies. It is similar to the NYSE.

New York Stock Exchange or NYSE: The most prestigious and oldest of all stock exchanges in the United States.

Non-qualified account: This is a standard investment account that doesn't "qualify" for any special tax treatments. These investment accounts are funded with after-tax dollars and are taxed annually. This is one of the most common types of investment accounts.

Options: These give the owner the option to purchase or sell a specific number of shares of a stock at a specific price. Options are bought and sold on the open market.

Penny stocks: Low-priced stocks, usually trade for less than $5 per share. They are not found on the major stock exchanges and usually carry high risk.

Preferred stock: Similar to common stock, but the owners have additional rights not given to owners of common stock. Among these rights is a first call on dividends.

Price/earnings ratio (P/E): This shows how a company's earnings relate to the stock price. The P/E is the current price of the stock divided by the annual earnings per share. The higher the P/E, the more earnings growth investors will expect.

Recession: An economic condition defined by a declining standard of living and rising prices. Technically, a recession is defined by a decline in the nation's gross national product for two consecutive quarters.

REIT: A real estate investment trust, or REIT, is a fund that purchases properties. The company that manages the fund takes care of maintaining the properties, managing, and renting them. A portion of the revenues is then distributed to shareholders who invested in the fund.

ROI or return on investment: A measure of how good the investment is or was. ROI is calculated by subtracting the cost of the investment from the gain of the investment. That total is then divided by the cost of the investment. For example, if you bought a house for $100,000 and sold it for $120,000, the ROI would be ($120,000 - $100,000)

/ $100,000 = 20%. Is 20 percent a good ROI? That really depends on how long it took to make that 20 percent.

Securities and Exchange Commission (SEC): This is the chief regulatory body over the stock markets and publicly traded companies.

Short selling: This is where an investor believes a stock is going to fall in price. The investor is able to borrow the stock from another client and then sell it. If the investor is correct, they would then buy the stock at the lower price, keep the difference, and then give the stock back to the person from whom they borrowed it.

Small cap stock: This type of stock is any company with a market capitalization of $1 billion or less.

Tax-loss harvesting: This is when a security is sold at a loss to offset a capital gain. It is typically used to limit recognizing short-term capital gains because these gains are usually taxed at higher rates (ordinary income).

Technical analysis: A form of stock evaluation that relies on stock data to predict future price trends. Technical analysis does not consider the business itself, but focuses strictly on the numbers, using quantitative data to drive decisions.

Tenants in common: This account title defines the ownership percentage of two or more parties on an account. Each person holds their own interest in the property, which can be unequal.

UTMA/UGMA: The Uniform Transfers/Gifts to Minors Act allows a minor to receive money in form of gifts. A custodian is named on behalf of the minor to manage the money on their behalf. Upon the child becoming age of majority (age eighteen in most states), the property will be transferred to them outright.

Wash sale: This typically happens when a security is sold for a loss and then repurchased within thirty days. If this happens, the original sale for the loss will no longer be deductible.

Wrap fee: This is a fee charged by a financial advisor for asset management services. The fee will usually include all costs associated with an investment account, including trading costs and advice. There are no commissions, rather the annual fee "wraps" all the advisor's services together.

Value stocks: These stocks are known for paying dividends, and often considered safer because of the "phase" the company is in. They are typically well-established companies.

Yield: The annual return of a stock, bond, or any investment expressed as a percentage of its cost.

Too many investors treat stock investing like gambling. The most successful investors avoid treating their investments like lottery tickets. Receiving a good return on your stock investments requires regular research.

It's difficult to understand any business without understanding how the company actually makes money. What are the sources of cash flow? Are those sources durable? Is the company likely to continue making money in all market conditions? For example, everyone still buys toilet paper and gasoline in a struggling economy. However, recreational vehicle sales tend to fall in the same market conditions. How long is the income stream likely to last? Is it dependent on technology or products that go out of date quickly?

In some industries, there's room for many competitors. Other industries are far more limited. Find the competitors. By researching the industry as a whole, it's quite easy to create a list of competing companies. Consider the revenue stream of your company's competitors. It's likely to be similar but not identical. You'll learn a lot by exploring the competition.

There's no shortage of free tools available to research financial data for any security. If you have a brokerage account, start there. A quick search will turn up numerous other options. You should make it a point to understand revenue, earnings per share, price to earnings ratio (P/E ratio), and return on investment. All of these terms have been defined above.

Whenever a company executive sells or purchases stock, that information must be made available to the public. Those executives are interested in making money. If they're buying the company's stock, that's a good sign. If they are selling, there could be a potential for concern.

Multiple authorities follow every significant industry. What are these experts saying? Avoid looking at just the recommendations. Dig in to the reasons for their opinions. It's a great way to learn. Keep in mind that the experts can be wrong. Avoid accepting any advice blindly. Check the information for yourself. Does it make sense? What factors are relevant? Don't react to what you hear on the news. Most of the time, it's too late.

If you are not completely sure if you should buy a stock, then don't. If you have any doubts, gather more information or research another stock. Make it a point to follow up periodically on all the stocks you research and see if your conclusions were correct. While it can be fun to try to pick your own stocks, it's wise to work with a professional.

Bond Terms

Coupon: The interest rate the bond pays. This interest rate is usually fixed over the life of the bond. However, there are also bonds with variable interest rates that are tied to an external index.

Current yield: The yield based on the current market price of that bond.

Face value/par value: Also called the face or principal value of the bond. The owner of the bond is given the face value upon the maturity of the bond.

Maturity: Refers to the length of time until the face value is received. This period of time may be a few months or as long as fifty years.

Yield to maturity: This calculation uses the current market price, interest rate, and time to maturity, and assumes that the interest payments received are reinvested at the bond's coupon rate. Also referred to as a bond's "yield." Yield to maturity calculations are extremely valuable because they include all the pertinent information and thus allow comparisons to be made between bond investments.

Zero coupon bonds: These don't provide periodic interest payments. Instead, they are sold at a discount. The only payment the investor receives is the face value at the end of maturity.

Bonds can be used for a variety of reasons, and they can be a bit complicated. While people tend to view bonds as boring, they can be a very useful investment vehicle. They can be used for saving money, generating income, managing risk, or tax planning. They're much more versatile than many investors give them credit for. It's worth spending some extra time getting to know them better.

Take a look at what bonds can do for you:

1. **Principal preservation.** This may be the most common use of bonds. This purpose most frequently makes use of short-term, very low-risk bonds, such as treasury bills. Low-risk bonds are a very effective way of transporting your money through time. while you won't make a lot of money, you'll still get some return. Many companies invest in bonds as a means of storing their money until some specific date in the future when they can better use it.

2. **Interest-rate risk management.** While this is a more complex use of bonds, bonds can be used to hedge against expected changes in interest rates. A portfolio of well-selected bonds can help you make money whether interest rates are falling or rising.

3. **Savings bonds.** There is a reason federal savings bonds are called savings bonds. They are one of the lowest-risk ways to save money for the long-term. The federal government guarantees them, with a wide range of options available. These options include bonds that pay interest, discount bonds, and more.

4. **Diversification.** Bonds are an effective diversification strategy; they tend to move in the other direction from other investments (negative correlation). So when your stocks go down, bonds tend to do favorably. Higher-risk bonds can also give high rates of return. Of course, you need to feel comfortable with the

risk—that the potential reward is worth your risk of loss. Junk bonds are not for the weak of heart.

5. **Plan for future expenses.** You can also use bonds to match future known expenses, like college tuition. For example, if you know you're going to need $25,000 ten years from now, you can buy a bond (or bonds) that will provide $25,000 in ten years.

6. **Income.** Unlike most stocks, bonds can provide a reliable and predictable stream of income over a long period of time. As you get closer to retirement age, it might make sense for you to consider moving a share of your portfolio into bonds. Companies such as insurance companies and banks rely on bonds for a large part of their income. In fact, insurance companies tend to pay out as much on claims as they earn in premiums. Their real income is typically from their investments, a large portion of which are bonds.

It's important to remember that bonds are not without risk, but the risk can be very minimal with the right homework. Understand a bond's risk rating before investing your money.

Mutual Fund Terms

Closed-end fund: A type of fund that issues a finite number of shares that trade throughout the day on stock exchanges at market-determined prices. Investors in a closed-end fund can buy or sell shares through a broker or online. Using this kind of fund is no different than buying and selling stock shares of any publicly traded company.

Expense ratio: The total of a fund's expenses, shown as a percentage of its assets. These expenses include operating expenses, salaries, and more, and amount to most of the cost of owning shares of that fund.

Front-end load: A fee that some funds impose at the time of purchase, in addition to the ongoing management expenses.

Hybrid fund: A mutual fund that invests in both stocks and bonds.

Money market fund: A mutual fund that invests in short term securities. Money market funds are very safe since the investments they make are quite low risk. Many people use these in lieu of a savings account. Money market funds are also a common place to hold money between investments.

Net asset value (NAV): The per-share value of a mutual fund. This is determined by subtracting the fund's liabilities from its assets and holdings and then dividing by the number of shares outstanding. This is calculated once a day after the market closes.

No-load fund: A mutual fund that is sold without a sales commission and doesn't have a 12b-1 charge of more than 0.25 percent per year. (See below for definition of 12b-1 fees.)

Open-end fund: A mutual fund that sells shares directly to investors. The fund also buys back shares when investors decide to sell. The price of the shares is always the net asset value (NAV).

Prospectus: Mutual funds have to provide an official document that describes the mutual fund to prospective investors. The information is required by the SEC and contains such attributes as policies, fees, and risks.

Total net assets: This is simply the total amount of assets a fund possesses minus its liabilities.

Total return: A measure of a fund's performance that considers all aspects of return—capital gains distributions, dividends, and changes in net asset value. The total return is assessed over a specific period of time and assumes that all dividends and capital gains distributions are reinvested.

Yield: A measure of income (dividends and interest) earned by the securities in a fund's portfolio minus the fund's expenses during a specified period. A fund's yield is expressed as a percentage of the maximum offering price per share on a specified date.

12b-1 fee: A mutual fund fee named for the SEC rule that permits it, used to pay distribution costs. One example of these expenses is compensation to financial advisors for initial and ongoing assistance. If a fund has a 12b-1 fee, it will be disclosed in the fee table of a fund's prospectus.

Real Estate Terms

Real estate can be a fantastic investment. It is often thought that a person's home is their most valuable tangible asset. While from a monetary value standpoint this might be true, the "money pit" of home ownership defies this principle. This is not to say you shouldn't own a home, but it shouldn't be classified as an investment. Owning a rental property to generate income is a phenomenal diversifier to have in your portfolio.

Acceleration clause: This is a clause in your mortgage that allows the lender to call the remaining principal of the loan due under certain circumstances. The most common reason for this occurring is if the borrower defaults on the loan.

Adjustable-rate mortgage (ARM): A mortgage in which the interest changes periodically. The interest rate is tied to a specified index.

Amortization: Your mortgage payment is applied to two things: the interest and the principal. As the loan is paid down, the interest portion of the payment decreases, and the portion used toward the principal increases.

Annual percentage rate (APR): This is the true cost of your mortgage, and takes into account all expenses. The APR includes fees and points, as well as the interest rate of your mortgage. Your APR is always higher than the interest rate of your mortgage. Also, it will tell you what your effective interest rate is, allowing easy comparison to other loan options.

Assumable mortgage: A mortgage that can be assumed by the buyer when then home is sold. There is usually a qualification process for the new owner before he or she can assume the mortgage.

Balloon mortgage: A mortgage that has a large final payment due at some point. For example, a loan may be amortized over a thirty-year period, but at ten years the remaining principle must be paid in full.

Closing: This will mean different things in different states. In many states, a real estate transaction is not "closed" until the documents are recorded at the recorder's office. In others, the "closing" is the meeting at which the documents are signed and funds are exchanged.

Closing costs: These are separated into either non-recurring closing costs or prepaid items. Non-recurring closing costs are items that are incurred only once as a result of buying the property or obtaining a loan. Prepaid items are those that recur over time, like homeowners insurance and property taxes. To the best of the lender's ability, these non-recurring closing costs and prepaid items are shown on the good faith estimate (GFE) that they're required to provide to the borrower within three days of receiving the mortgage application.

Deed: The legal document that conveys title to a property.

Equal Credit Opportunity Act (ECOA): A federal law that requires lenders and other creditors to make credit equally available without discrimination based on race, color, religion, national origin, age, sex, marital status, or receipt of income from public assistance programs.

Equity: The difference between the fair market value of the property and the amount owed on the mortgage and other liens. To the owner, it is essentially the amount of net worth in the home.

First mortgage: The mortgage that is in the preferential position among all the loans recorded against that property. This is the loan that would get paid first if the house were foreclosed and auctioned off. Normally, this is the loan that is recorded first, which is why it is commonly referred to as a first mortgage.

Fixed-rate mortgage: A mortgage in which the interest rate is fixed throughout the life of the loan.

Good faith estimate (GFE): This estimate is required by law to be provided to a potential mortgage customer within three days of applying for a loan. The GFE must include an itemized list of all fees and costs associated with that loan. These fees include things like inspections, title insurance, and taxes.

Home equity loan: A loan secured against a property that allows the borrower to obtain money drawn against home's equity. Usually such a loan is in second position (after the first mortgage).

Loan-to-value ratio (LTV): The amount of the loan divided by either the appraised value or sales price (whichever is lower). This value is one of the factors used to determine if a loan would be approved.

Note: Any legal document that obligates a borrower to repay a mortgage loan at a specified interest rate over a specified period of time.

PITI (principal, interest, taxes and insurance): Your mortgage payment may include all of these, depending on the terms of the loan. Taxes are frequently placed into an escrow account, and the lender applies the funds toward property taxes.

Points: Points are essentially fees that the borrower must pay to receive a home loan. One point would equal one percent of the loan amount. By paying more points up front, a lower interest rate can usually be obtained.

Prime rate: The short-term interest rate used by banks. The prime rate serves as the index in some adjustable rate mortgages and home equity lines of credit. You'll see the prime rate mentioned in the newspaper and on TV all the time. This number is invaluable. When the prime rate is rising, you can expect mortgage rates will eventually rise as well. Variables that influence the prime rate will usually affect the interest rates of new fixed mortgages. The prime rate is usually the Fed's funds target rate plus 3 percent. Many interest rates used by the bank are a function of the prime rate.

Principal: The amount of money borrowed or the amount that remains unpaid. When you get a home loan for $100,000, the principal is $100,000. The principal can also refer to that portion of a loan payment that is applied to the principal balance of the loan.

Private mortgage insurance (PMI): This is mortgage insurance provided by a private mortgage insurance company. PMIs insure lenders in the event that the borrower doesn't pay. Most lenders generally require PMI for all loans where to loan-to-value (LTV) percentage is greater than 80 percent.

Qualifying ratios: Lending institutions use several ratios to decide whether a borrower can qualify for a mortgage. The two ratios primarily used are the "top" or "front" ratio and the "back" or "bottom" ratio. The top ratio is a calculation of the borrower's total monthly housing costs (mortgage payment, taxes, insurance, mortgage insurance, etc.) divided by monthly income. The bottom ratio includes housing costs and also all other monthly debt. These ratios are very important to lenders.

There are several ways to invest in real estate. You can own your own properties and manage them or you can buy investments that own real estate, such as a real estate investment trust (REIT).

There are several advantages to adding shares of one or more publicly traded REITs to your portfolio:

1. **Passive income.** REITs provide you with a regular income without having to actively manage your investments.

2. **You can invest in multiple properties.** For example, you can find REITs that give you exposure to industrial real estate, commercial projects such as malls, office buildings, or residential buildings. Building such a diverse portfolio while actually holding properties is very difficult and takes years.

3. **High liquidity.** You can sell your shares or decide to invest in more at any time.

4. **Protection against high interest rates.** While products such as bonds typically lose some of their value when interest rates go up, REITs tend to gain value. High interest rates mean the economy is in good shape, which results in higher rent, higher occupancy rates for residential rental properties, and high demand for commercial and industrial properties.

5. **Ease of diversifying your portfolio.** The wide range of REITs makes it easy for you to build a diverse portfolio. You can invest in several different types of properties and gain exposure to real estate markets both in the country and abroad.

Not all REITs make a good addition to your portfolio, so you must take caution. Be sure to consider the following:

1. **Unprofitable locations of the properties.** Some REITs don't perform well due to poor location of the properties the fund invested in.

2. **Bad management.** Some bad management practices can result in loss of revenues. Ensure the fund you invest in includes properties that are actively managed and renters are treated fairly.

3. **Past profitability.** Check price and revenue history to get a better idea of how an REIT has been performing before you invest.

REITs can be a great addition to your portfolio if you want exposure to real estate markets without owning and managing a property. These funds are very accessible to novice investors, but it's important to select a fund that performs well.

Retirement and Education Terms

Retirement and education terms have been lumped together because these types of investments share many similarities. For both investments, it is frequently possible to make pre-tax contributions and/or take tax-free distributions. There are many ways you can save toward accomplishing your retirement and education goals. Understanding the differences of these types of investments will help you decide what's best for you.

401(k) plan: A retirement plan sponsored by employers. A 401(k) allows employees to make tax-deferred contributions directly from their salaries to the plan. Employers may match a certain percentage of the employee's contributions. It is strongly suggested that if you have an employer who provides a match, you should at a minimum contribute on your own up to the match percentage. This money is given to you! Who doesn't like free money?

403(b) plan: This is very similar to a 401(k) plan, but it applies to employees of public schools, universities, and nonprofit organizations.

457 plan: Again, similar to a 401(k), but applies only to employees of state and local governments.

529 plan: An investment program that is supported by state governments to help pay future qualified higher education expenses. Many states will offer a state tax deduction up to a maximum. The money invested in these plans will grow tax-deferred and can be used tax free for education expenses. While originally designed to pay for higher education, many states and plans now allow the use of these funds for secondary private schooling. If you take a distribution from a 529 plan and don't use it for a child's education, you may be assessed a 10 percent penalty. One nice feature of these plans is they will allow for a transfer to another family member. Some plans are even designed to be prepaid. This allows you to set aside funds and lock in the cost of education in present dollars.

Individual retirement account (IRA): An account by an individual to maintain and invest funds for retirement. Typically, the contributions are made by receiving a tax deduction for the year you make the contribution. The investments will grow tax-deferred while they are invested. Upon distribution of these assets, they will be taxed at your ordinary income tax rate. If you take a premature distribution (before you turn 59 ½) you could be subject to a 10 percent penalty in addition to the tax due. The IRS will require you to start taking a required minimum distribution at age seventy-two. The maximum contribution limits usually change each year, and those limits are increased if you are over the age of fifty. While almost anyone is eligible to participate in an IRA, it's important to note that above certain incomes, the deduction can become phased out. In this situation, the use of the IRA becomes less attractive.

Inherited IRA - IRA/BDA-: When a person passes away and owns an IRA, both the rules and how to handle the distribution could be extremely complex. The following are the basic rules and assumes the person passed away after January 1, 2020. If you inherit an IRA from your spouse, you can make a choice to rollover the funds into your own IRA and treat it as your own, or you can roll it into an inherited IRA like any other non-spouse would do. Depending on the option you choose, different rules for distribution would apply. If a non-spouse inherits an IRA from someone, they must withdraw the assets over a ten year time span following the year of death of the original account holder. As with many other things, there are exceptions to this rule. In either case of a spouse or non-spouse, if you negelct to take the required distribution, a penalty can be assessed. Consider consulting with both a tax and investment professional, as this can get complicated.

Nondeductible IRA: Depending upon your income, you may not be eligible to participate in an IRA. This is called a phase-out. The IRS will allow you to make a nondeductible IRA contribution. While this seems great on the surface, it can cause a lot of confusion. One of the benefits of an IRA is the deductibility and the tax-deferred growth. When your contribution is not deductible, you will file a form with your tax return. This form helps you and the IRS keep track of the taxable and non-taxable portion of your account. This is where the trickiness comes in. When you start taking money from this account, the nondeductible principal will come back to you tax free, but you will have to pay ordinary income tax on all the gains. It is much easier to avoid this situation by using a backdoor Roth (explained below).

Keogh: This is a plan very similar to a 401(k), but it is for self-employed individuals, partners, and owners of unincorporated businesses. It is sometimes referred to as an H.R. 10 plan. You very rarely see these implemented anymore.

Qualified retirement plan: These are plans that are acknowledged and authorized by the IRS and required to follow specific rules and regulations. Participants may accumulate money in these accounts on a tax-deferred basis. IRAs and 401(k)s are examples of qualified retirement plans.

Required minimum distribution: In general, holders of traditional IRAs must begin withdrawing money from the account in the year you turn age seventy-two. The amount required is a minimum distribution determined by your age and life expectancy. The IRS has tables available to determine the required withdrawal. If required withdrawals are not made on time, the IRS will collect an excise tax. Roth IRAs aren't subject to minimum distribution requirements until after the Roth owner dies.

Rollover: Under certain circumstances—when changing jobs, for instance—an investor may transfer funds from one qualified retirement account to another. This may be done without a tax penalty. It is important to note that you are entitled to make only one rollover in any given twelve-month period. A plan partipant leaving an employer typicaly has four options (and may engage in a combination of these options). Each choice offers advantages and disadvantages. These options are:

1. Leave the money in his/her former employer's plan, if permitted.

2. Roll over the assets to his/her new employer's plan, if one is available and rollovers are permitted.

3. Roll over to an IRA; or

4. Cash out the account value.

Roth IRA: Roth IRAs were first available in 1998. This IRA only allows after-tax contributions, but the earnings aren't taxed. Provided the guidelines are followed, all distributions are tax free. The Roth IRA is an excellent tool because of its tax treatment. There is the potential of being phased out of this as well depending upon your income. The good news is there is something called a "backdoor Roth."

Backdoor Roth: If you find yourself in a situation where your income is too high to contribute to a Roth IRA, don't worry, you're in luck. While it could be a bit tricky, here's how you can accomplish receipt of the Roth IRA benefits. If you establish a traditional IRA, you will make a nondeductible contribution. As early as the very next day, you can do a "Roth conversion" of those funds by transferring the money into the Roth IRA account. Then you would invest money within the Roth account.

It is important to note that while you can do this on your own, it can be quite complicated. It is always best to work with a qualified tax professional and financial planner to help you with these advanced planning concepts.

Trustee-to-trustee transfer: Unlike a rollover that can be done only once per year, a trustee-to-trustee transfer can be done without limit. This is simply moving one retirement account from one financial institution to the next. For example, if you have an IRA with multiple investment companies, you may wish to combine them. If an electronic transfer is completed, or a check made payable directly to another financial institution for your benefit, it is considered a transfer, not a rollover.

If you are self-employed you can use your business to help you save for your retirement.

Thankfully, the retirement contribution limits can be higher for the self-employed than for those working for companies. The contribution limit amounts will usually adjust higher for inflation. You will want to check each year to see what the limits are.

Primary retirement accounts for the self-employed include:

1. **SEP-IRA.** SEP stands for "simplified employee pension." This is a great bet if you're working solo. The government is kind enough to allow you to save and invest up to 25 percent of your self-employment net income. The maximum amount permitted is $57,000 in 2020.

   - In a SEP-IRA, the money is pre-tax and can therefore reduce your tax burden. If you have employees, then you're required to contribute money for them as well.

   - The plan doesn't have to be funded until your taxes are filed, which provides incredible flexibility. You can wait until the last minute to decide how much you're going to put into the account. This is handy if you find yourself owing more or less in taxes than you originally expected.

2. **Keogh plan.** This plan is essentially a self-funded pension plan. Keogh plans have an annual contribution limit of $57,000 for 2020. Since the paperwork to set up the plan is arduous and Solo 401(k) plans also offer the same generous contribution limits, Keogh plans have fallen out of favor.

3. **Solo 401(k).** This is a great way to save a lot of money for retirement. It's a highly flexible plan with a maximum contribution of 20 percent of your net self-employment income plus $19,500. The total maximum is $57,000 for 2020 plus an additional $6,500 if you are age fifty or older. While it's necessary to establish a Solo 401(k) account during the tax year, it doesn't have to be funded until your taxes are filed.

4. **SIMPLE IRA.** This is a viable solution for those with employees or those who work alone. The Savings Incentive Match Plan for Employees is an incredibly easy plan to set up. Completing the IRS form 5305-Simple and opening an account are the only required steps. The annual maximum is $13,500 per year for those under fifty. Fifty or older, $16,500. The account must be opened by October 1 of each year. If you have employees, you're obligated to match their

contributions up to 3 percent. (There are exceptions to this 3 percent rule)

Deciding on the best plan could be confusing. In many cases, a SIMPLE IRA is best for those without employees and with incomes of $50,000 or less, whereas a Solo 401(k) or SEP-IRA will allow those with higher incomes to save more.

Make the decision to invest regularly in your retirement. Income for the self-employed can be less consistent. Avoid assuming that you'll have the money available in later years.

Consider the adage, "Pay yourself first." It's much easier to save for retirement if money is set aside each month, rather than simply saving whatever funds remain at the end of the year. There rarely seems to be anything left with that strategy.

Many business owners believe they can fund their retirement by selling their business. Perhaps they can, but it isn't a certainty. Better safe than sorry. Take the time today to develop a retirement strategy that will serve you well in your retirement years. It's doubtful you'll regret saving, but you'll probably regret it if you don't.

Putting This into Practice

Now that you understand the many investment products and plan types available, you can start planning on where and how you want to start investing. Even if you have very little to invest now, it's important to start as early as possible. The sooner you begin, the sooner you can build wealth by increasing your assets. Remember, investing even a small amount of money may earn you a higher return than doing nothing at all.

When investing, long-term investment gains can transform a modest five-figure investment into a six-figure return. Long-term interest compounds quickly. Assuming you were to invest $25,000 today and your investment earned 8 percent, one year later you will have $27,000. Though a $2,000 return may seem modest, this is actually a great return. When gains compound each year, your initial $25,000 can turn into much, much more.

The examples shown in the charts below showcase two initial investments, one of $25,000 and another of $75,000 showing gains over a ten-year time span. Both examples are based on an 8 percent rate of return.

As you'll see, in the first example your investment has more than doubled in ten years. With gains alone, you've earned $28,968! In the second example, your larger investment has more than doubled as well. In this case you have gains of $86,914! If building long-term wealth is your goal, growth-oriented investment options should be considered.

Example 1:

Initial Investment: $25,000		
Investment	Interest	Year-end Total
$25,000	8%	$27,000
$27,000	8%	$29,160
$29,160	8%	$31,492
$31,492	8%	$34,012
$34,012	8%	$36,732
$36,732	8%	$39,670
$39,670	8%	$42,843
$42,843	8%	$46,270
$46,270	8%	$49,971
$49,971	8%	$53,968

Example 2:

Initial Investment: $75,000		
Investment:	Interest:	Year-end Total
$75,000	8%	$81,000
$81,000	8%	$87,480
$87,480	8%	$94,478
$94,478	8%	$102,036
$102,036	8%	$110,198
$110,198	8%	$119,013
$119,013	8%	$128,534
$128,534	8%	$138,816
$138,816	8%	$149,921
$149,921	8%	$161,914

These are hypothetical examples and are not representative of any specific investment. These examples shows a fixed 8% interest rate to illustrate the power of compound interest.

Clearly, you've seen the benefits associated with long-term investments. Rather than making quick money, you're able to build true wealth by making calculated long-term investments that may eventually lead to a high return by the power of compound interest (investment growth).

One of the most asked questions is "What's a good rate of return?" The answer is, it depends! As discussed multiple times, every person's situation is unique and must be examined on an individual basis. That said, when it comes to rate of return, it's paramount you understand variance of return. When judging performance, one of the most critical aspects to examine is timing. You and someone else could have the exact same investments in your portfolio, but if one person invested in one year and someone else invested a year later, the results can be dramatically different.

In addition, times of loss are much more detrimental to a portfolio than most would think, especially if you are retired and taking distributions. Assuming you had $100,000 in a portfolio and you lost 50 percent in one year, how much would you have at the end of that year- $50,000, right? Now, what rate of return would you need in order to get back to the $100,000 you started with? That's right, 100 percent! You need to double your upside to earn back your losses. For this reason, the concept of building a portfolio having the understanding of upside/ downside capture will be most beneficial. While your portfolio value will fluctuate up and down, you should focus on doing your best to curtail downside loss.

Below is a hypothetical example of two asset managers. Review the performance of each and decide which money manager would be right for you and why.

Year	Manager A	Manager B
1	22%	9%
2	40%	9%
3	20%	9%
4	-50%	9%
5	38%	9%
	14% — Average Annual Return —	9%

What manager did you choose? If you chose manager A, you probably focused on percentages alone and looked at the bottom-line average. You may be thinking how we have been discussing long-term investing and why not take more risk to have more money in the end, right? Hold that thought. If you decided on manager B, you probably did so because you wanted consistency and weren't too focused on percentages. Now let's look at what this scenario looks like when we use dollars and cents.

	Manager A		Manager B	
Year				
1	22%	$100,000	9%	$100,000
2	40%	$122,000	9%	$109,000
3	20%	$171,000	9%	$119,000
4	-50%	$205,000	9%	$129,000
5	38%	$103,000	9%	$141,000
		$142,000		$154,000

7.3%	Compounded Portfolio Return	9%

So, what manager do you want now, and why? You may be surprised to see how this actually works out when you insert dollars and cents and not focus on average return. One might argue that manager A did better for the first three years, and that is correct. However, to be successful, the investor would've needed a crystal ball or get extremely lucky getting out in year three. That said, what this won't take into account is when they would decide to get back in.

The point here is while scenario B is highly unlikely (to earn 9 percent every single year), the closer you can build a portfolio to resemble this manager, the better. Focusing on rates of return is only as important as it is to what you are trying to accomplish personally. It is not advisable to try to time the market, because it usually will not work. Staying the course and trying to earn consistent returns and limit the downside based on your individual time horizon and risk tolerance is the key to realizing your own personal investment goals.

Selecting an investment professional is always advisable. While you may have some success on your own, an investment advisor should help you make suitable investment decisions. Also, investment advisors manage your assets, explain the nuances of the various vehicles available for investing, and show you investment strategies that are customized for you.

Investment advisors make their suggestions based upon your goals, budget, comfort levels with risk, and time frame. While a financial planner charges fees, they can save you thousands by simply directing you away from mistakes, rather than allowing you to learn the hard (and rather expensive) way.

A financial planner will get paid through an up-front fee, hourly wage, or percentage of your asset management. Some advisors may also make commissions on the products they recommend. Always ask your advisor up front how they get paid.

It's important to select an advisor you're comfortable with. A lack of experience can alter your financial future in a negative way. As mentioned in the past, while credentials aren't necessary to be an investment advisor, it is recommended you work with someone who focuses on planning and has the appropriate credentials of such.

Below are some general guidelines you should consider before putting your money to work.

1. **Know your starting point.** Before starting any race, you have to know where the starting line is located. Take regular measurements of your financial situation to gauge your progress. Know the difference between your basis (what you started with) and where you are today.

2. **Avoid investing in a business or financial instrument you aren't able to understand.** If you're unclear about the fundamentals of an investment, how will you know if it's a good investment or if and when you should sell it? For example, if you lack an understanding of derivative products, that would be a good reason to stay away from investing in them.

3. **Try not to invest and forget.** Most investments require regular monitoring and assessment. Market conditions can change, so try to remember to check on all your investments. Company situations change all the time—change of management, taking on debt, new products, etc. Any of these can change performance instantly! Stay on top of the latest news and make any necessary adjustments to your investments. At a minimum, you should consider rebalancing quarterly to maintain your objectives.

4. **Look past the price and the past returns.** The real value of an investment isn't always evident by looking at the price or past performance. Take the time to dig in and see if an investment has real value. For example, perhaps an investment is underpriced because it's a great buy. However, maybe it's underpriced because the investment is having issues.

5. **Remember to consider inflation.** Most investors forget to consider the effects of inflation when choosing investments. Investing is looking toward the future, so inflation is an important consideration.

6. **Make tax planning an ongoing process.** Most people plan for taxes only at tax time. However, the wise investor considers tax issues throughout the entire year. Whenever you make an investment, consider what the tax implications might be. A little bit of forethought can mean thousands of dollars during tax time. Employing tax-loss-harvesting strategies is a must.

7. **Retirement savings should take precedence.** When retirement savings isn't a priority, you usually won't have much of a retirement fund. We're all prone to putting things off until tomorrow. Make your retirement a priority, and you may live comfortably in your golden years.

Investing can be complex, and it does require discipline and planning. These general guidelines should help provide a framework that will allow you to stay on track.

In conclusion, whether you have $1,000 or $100,000, investing is a solid step toward your financial independence. There are many components to investing. It takes time, experience, education, and just a bit of money to start. It may be even better with the help of the right professional. With the knowledge you have now, you're already off to a productive start.

Note: All investing involves risk including the possible loss of principal. No strategy assures success or protects against loss.

There is no guarantee that a diversified portfolio will enhance overall returns or outperform a non-diversified portfolio. Diversifcation does not protect against market risk.

ETFs trade like stocks, are subject to investment risk, fluctuate in market value, and may trade at prices above or below the ETFs net asset value (NAV). Upon redemption, the value of fund shares may be worth more or less than their original cost. ETFs carry addtional risks such as not being diversified, possible trading halts, and index tracking errors.

Dividend payments are not guaranteed and may be reduced or eliminated at any time by the company.

Dollar cost averaging involves continuous investment in securities regardless of fluctuation in price levels of such securities. An investor should consider their ability to continue purchasing through fluctuating price levels. Such a plan does not assure a profit and does not protect against loss in declining markets.

Bonds are subject to market and interest rate risk if sold prior to maturity. Bond values will decline as interest rates rise and bonds are subject to availability and change in price.

Investing in Real Estate Investment Trusts (REITs) involves special risks such as potential illiquidity and may not be suitable for all investors. There is no assurance that the investment objectives of this program will be attained.

Rebalancing a portfolio may cause investors to incur tax liabilities and/or transaction costs, and does not assure a profit or portect against a loss.

INVESTMENT WORKSHEET

With the knowledge you have now, answer the following questions to gain a personal perspective of your investment plans. Take your time completing this before shelling out your hard-earned money.

1. Have I set aside funds to pursue my goals? If no, how much do I need to save in order to get the ball rolling?

_____

_____

_____

_____

2. How will I allocate the funds to make my first investment? If I must adjust my household budget, what areas of my current expenses will have to be trimmed?

_____

_____

_____

3. Have I determined how I will invest my money? If so, what is my strategy?

_____

_____

_____

_____

_____

4. Am I willing to speak to an investment advisor in order to gain a professional perspective on my current strategy? What questions will I ask him/her to ensure we're a good fit?

_____

_____

_____

_____

5. How do I plan to educate myself on my investment of choice before investing my hard-earned cash?

_____

_____

_____

_____

6. Am I investing for the long or short term? What kind of return do I expect and why?

_____

_____

_____

_____

_____

7. Do I have enough information to decide as to whether a tax-preferred, traditional, or both investment types aligns best with my goals? What information do I need?

_____

_____

_____

_____

_____

8. Do I know how to analyze the performance of my investments? What key metrics do I need to pay particular attention to?

_____

_____

_____

_____

9. Do I have a plan B in case my first plan falls short? What is it?

_____

_____

_____

_____

_____

_____

_____

THE ASSET DISTRIBUTION COMPONENT

Who doesn't want to retire comfortably? After working your entire life, it's now time to enjoy yourself. Even if you've made smart financial decisions all the way up to retirement, it's still possible to make mistakes that can derail your goals and dreams. The responsibility you have to yourself and your family doesn't change when you retire. In fact, you need to be just as diligent, if not more, to ensure you never run out of money.

Income during your retirement can be generated from many areas. If you have done proper planning, you should have several "buckets" of money to access. A distribution strategy is extremely important, especially considering you more than likely have accumulated assets that are taxed differently. In addition, as you get older, your tolerance for risk may have changed. Consistent analysis of your portfolio will be even more crucial than ever. If you were dollar cost averaging into your portfolio while you were accumulating assets, now you have the opposite. Reverse dollar cost averaging (taking money out each month) could be catastrophic without consistent portfolio review. If you are taking monthly distributions and then have a severe market downturn simultaneously, it makes the chances for recovery much more challenging.

You must always continue to educate yourself. The laws and rules around retirement accounts, taxes, investing, and Social Security regularly change.

The key to achieving financial stability is to make your money last. Life expectancy continues to rise. Can you afford to stay in retirement if you live to your eighties, nineties, or beyond? This is an important question that requires careful thought and planning along with review of your goals, insurance, and cash flow. Has anything changed?

A list of your retirement goals can help you figure out how to stay financially stable. Each goal has a financial value. Consider how you can safely work each goal into your financial plan based on the money you've saved and the income sources you will now have. While goals are great, don't forget about the essentials. Retirement essentials are basic housing, food, medications, and other necessary costs. All of these are tied to your financial stability.

Too many retirees realize they haven't saved enough for their retirement until it's too late. They rely too heavily on

Social Security as a main source of income. While it helps, it is definitely not enough.

Almost everyone has questions concerning Social Security. Most likely, you aren't really sure how much money you'll get or when you'll start getting it. It's difficult to plan for your retirement when you don't know the details surrounding Social Security.

Common Questions about Social Security

1. **When do I start receiving payments?**

   It depends on when you were born:

   • Prior to 1938? Your date of full eligibility is sixty-five.

   • If you were born after 1960, the date is age sixty-seven.

   • For everyone else, it is between age sixty-five and age sixty-seven.

2. **Am I eligible?**

   You must earn forty credits to receive Social Security. In 2011, a credit is earned for every $1,120 of earned income. A maximum of four credits can be earned per year. So, you would have to earn approximately

$4,500 a year for ten years to be eligible at the current credit rates.

3. How much money will I get?

The rate is determined by averaging your earnings over your thirty-five highest income years.

4. Can I still receive Social Security if I'm still earning?

Provided that you've reached full retirement age, you can receive full payments without penalty. If you decide to start receiving Social Security early, you can earn up to $18,240 (2020) without penalty. If you go past that limit, you'll lose $1 for every $2 earned beyond the limit.

5. What about my spouse?

If your spouse did not earn enough money over their lifetime to qualify for benefits that are equivalent to at least half of yours, their benefits will be set equal to half of your benefit.

6. What if my spouse dies?

In the event that your spouse dies, you're entitled to their full benefit amount, provided that you've already reached retirement age yourself. If you haven't reached retirement age, you'll receive a prorated amount.

7. **Is the current Social Security system in trouble?**

It's not as healthy as it could be. For the time being, the system is okay. However, as the number of people retiring increases relative to the number of people working, it could be in trouble without changes. Additionally, people are living longer, which further stretches the system.

8. **Isn't all the money we are paying into the system being saved and invested?**

No. The money paid into the system isn't put into a separate account. It's commingled with all the other money the IRS collects from us. The money is spent on all government expenditures, including highways, schools, and the military. The idea that Social Security taxes are spent only on Social Security payments is a myth.

9. **Will there be money left when I retire?**

The consensus is the system will not be allowed to fail. However, it's likely that many changes will have to be made in the future. An example of one change that has already been made is changing the full retirement age from sixty-five to sixty-seven.

Maximizing your Social Security benefits is important. Here are some mistakes you want to avoid:

1. **Avoid claiming benefits too early.** If you have other income coming in and can afford to wait, then you may want delay claiming your benefits. Your benefits grow every year you wait to claim them. By claiming benefits early, you reduce how much money you will receive for the rest of your retirement. However, it's important to note that sometimes claiming early benefits can be more advantageous than waiting. For example, if you're expecting a shorter life span, you might want to start receiving your Social Security earnings early. Or, if you have children under eighteen years old when you're sixty-two, you may get more by claiming early.

    It's always good to check your estimated benefits on the calculators at the Social Security website at https://www.socialsecurity.gov/planners/benefitcalculators.html.

2. **Consider the tax implications.** Are you aware that Social Security benefits can be taxed? It's a common mistake to forget the tax implications of Social Security benefits. This is called the Social Security Tax Torpedo. Your benefits can be taxed at a high rate, and it can last for your entire retirement. Your total income affects the tax rate you'll be subject to.

3. **Consider the total years you've worked.** Social Security looks at thirty-five years of earnings to determine benefits. Have you worked for thirty-five years? They use the income from your highest-earning thirty-five years, indexed for inflation, to figure out what your average yearly income was. Generally, the longer your record, the higher your benefits.

4. **Check your records each year.** As you work on your taxes, you may want to use this time as a reminder to check your Social Security records. It's possible for your records to have missing information or errors. Social Security gives you three years to fix an error on the record. After this time, it may be impossible to fix.

5. **Consider your partner's income.** Have you considered your partner's retirement and Social Security benefits? If your partner earns significantly more than you do, you might be able to collect higher benefits based on your partner's earnings.

6. **Consider the maximum benefit.** Each year, Social Security has a cap on the amount of income that you pay Social Security taxes on. If you earn a high income, some of your income-producing years might exceed the limit, and the excess income won't be used in figuring your average income amount. You can find these limits on the official website.

Social Security can be an essential part of your retirement plans. Use these strategies to avoid mistakes that can cost you money in your retirement

In conclusion, when employment income is no longer sufficient, the money needed to maintain lifestyle needs to come from somewhere. While some people are fortunate to receive pensions, the majority of people don't receive one. The benefit of both Social Security and pension income is the consistency. Like a paycheck, you know how much you will receive each month. When you rely solely or even partially on investment income, it's not as simple. There are too many unknown variables that can affect an investment account to generate a guaranteed income stream. Proper planning and being strategic with investment accounts is critical to avoid running out of money.

Annuities - They may not be so bad after all

In a prior chapter it was discussed why annuities receive such a bad reputation. For the right person, and in the right circumstance, they can be extremely beneficial. The issue is some people get "sold" these products when they don't need it. Modern-day annuities can offer attractive benefits to help provide a guaranteed income stream during retirement. For those who don't have pensions, this could be a worthwhile strategy. There are so many different types of annuities that exist today and a plethora of issuers too. Therefore, you need to educate yourself on what's available and how these contracts work. If you think this strategy might work for you, it's important the advisor you work with understands your entire plan.

Remember, if your withdrawals are too small, you'll have lived more frugally than necessary. But, if you withdraw too much money, then you may exhaust your funds. Utilizing an annuity strategy within your plan can help solve this. Again, assuming you have clearly identified your cash flow and goals.

Below are some basic annuity income concepts you should understand before even starting a conversation about purchasing one of these products.

The strategies below relate to annuitization options. *This is the process of choosing an income stream over a specified period of time that is most appropriate to your situation.* They can be used on fixed annuities (money tied to an interest rate) or variable (money invested in mutual funds).

1. **Life income option.** This annuitization option guarantees you income for the rest of your life, regardless of how long you live! In essence, you're guaranteed to never run out of money as long as the company issuing the annuity is in business. Your income depends on your age when you start the payout phase to receive benefits and how much you invest into the annuity. An illustration can be provided to you showing the income generated. Although you'll have the peace of mind knowing you'll never run out of money, keep in mind that if

you die soon in the payout phase, the issuing company retains the rest of your funds, per your contract. This type of annuity is not very common anymore. Most people are not comfortable taking the chance that the insurance company will keep their money if they die prematurely. **Please note: there are annuities that provide lifetime income that will pay the remainder to a named beneficiary upon death of the annuitant (a person who receives an annuity).**

2. **Life option with a guaranteed term.** With this annuitization option, it is guaranteed that your benefits will be paid for at least a certain amount of time, such as ten or fifteen years (at a minimum) but continue for the rest of your life, even if there is nothing left in the balance of the underlying account. Your beneficiary will continue to receive funds for the remainder of the term if you should die before the term ends.

3. **Single premium immediate option.** You purchase this type of annuity with a single premium payment and start the payout phase immediately. In other words, when you retire, you can withdraw part of your savings and purchase an annuity with one payment. What's interesting about this single premium option is that if you also select the life income option at the time you paid your single premium, you can begin receiving annuity payments immediately that will continue to pay out for the rest of your life!

4. **Joint-life option.** This option is set up to consider both you and your spouse's life expectancies. Thus, the amount you'll receive will be less than what you receive in the regular life option (see #1). However, if you die, your annuity funds would pass directly to your spouse. Some annuity policies even allow for the beneficiary to continue placing money into the annuity, thus building the total amount to provide additional retirement funding later. In this case, the funds will last as long as your beneficiary chooses.

5. **Term certain option.** This type of annuitization enables you to specify the term you want to receive funds. Maybe you want to receive your annuity spread over fifteen years or even thirty years. The advantage of selecting a longer period or "term" to be paid is that your retirement dollars last longer. Another advantage of term certain annuities is that if you die early in the payment term (let's say you die the fifth year of a twenty-year payout term), your beneficiary will receive the remaining fifteen years of payouts.

Similar to other insurance products, many annuities offer riders. They are usually found on variable annuities, and the most common are living benefit riders known as guaranteed minimum income benefit (GMIB) or guaranteed minimum withdrawal benefit (GMWB) riders.

A GMIB is an optional rider that annuitants can purchase for their retirement annuities. This rider allows for the annuitant to take a lifetime income stream regardless of what the underlying investment account value is. This rider is used for someone who plans to annuitize their contract.

A **variable annuity** is invested in mutual funds. The income stream offered by this rider is usually based on the value of the underlying investment options or a stated minimum interest rate. This is attractive to investors because it gives them the opportunity to receive income if the account value grows, but also protects them if the market declines by reverting to the interest rate offered. Some riders will even provide for an income based on the highest account value the contract ever reached. For example, a GMIB rider may offer income based on the greater of market performance or a compounded 6 percent rate of return, whichever is greater. Or, they may provide income on the highest value the investments ever reached.

The GMIB is something to consider because of the income protection it can provide; however, this does come with a cost. These riders do cost money that will "eat away" at the market performance. That said, it could be thought of as buying an insurance policy on your investment account. These contracts are extremely complex, so it's important you understand them inside and out. Something else to consider is the choice of investment options. Sometimes, they could be limited. If you think this strategy could work for you, discuss it with a qualified advisor.

The GMWB rider is similar to the GMIB, although it doesn't force you to annuitize the contract. The withdrawal benefit will allow an income to be withdrawn against the contract value or a stated interest rate to create lifetime income. The rider will protect against investment losses while still offering significant potential for market growth. Many of these riders will allow a percentage of the account value to be withdrawn along with taking a portion of the increased investment value. This is a very flexible rider because the contract doesn't have be to be annuitized. These rider definitions vary from company to company, so you should learn about the differences.

For example, let's assume you made an investment of $100,000, and the rider allows for a 5 percent distribution stream. This would mean, regardless of market performance, you could withdraw $5,000 per year until you have recovered your initial investment, therefore protecting your principal. Some will even allow the $5,000 income to continue even beyond the initial investment. Assuming positive performance and it grew to $200,000, the company may allow you to withdraw the minimum 5 percent plus a percentage of the growth. This rider also costs money, but it could be worth the cost to have the protection and added flexibility.

With some forethought and proper strategic planning, you can set up an annuity to aid you in stretching your retirement dollars throughout your lifetime

While you're welcome to retire anywhere you want, where you choose to retire can have a significant effect on your finances and retirement lifestyle.

Selecting a state to live in for your retirement should depend on your level and sources of income. States have varying tax laws that can really make a difference in the amount of money you'll have left over at the end of each month.

During retirement, determining your best taxation situation depends on more than just seeing if your state has a state income tax or not. For example, your favorite state might have a state income tax, but not tax pension income. So, if pension income is your main source of income, it might still benefit you financially to consider that state.

Let's look at the four main taxes different states apply to varying degrees:

1. **Taxes on pension income.** Currently, there are only three states that don't tax pension income: Mississippi, Illinois, and Pennsylvania. If you have a military or government pension, there are several more tax-free options: New York, Michigan, Hawaii, Kansas, Louisiana, Massachusetts, and Alabama. Other states tax your pension income to varying degrees. Do your homework if you receive a pension as part of your retirement income.

2. **Sales taxes.** If you don't want to pay any sales tax, then Alaska, New Hampshire, Oregon, or Montana are your answer. Of course, sales tax rates vary from state to state. Also, some states exempt certain items like food, medical care, and medical supplies. Take a

look before you make the leap. The more you like to shop, the more sales tax will detract from your bottom line!

3. **Property taxes.** If you own an expensive home or multiple properties, property taxes can be significant. Property taxes are largely a function of property values, so you can limit your property taxes by living in an area with lower real estate prices. Keep in mind that city and local taxes can be a significant portion of property taxes. Find out what you can expect to pay in property taxes before you choose your retirement location. In certain areas, it might even make sense to rent instead of own property.

4. **Taxes on Social Security benefits.** There are thirty-six states (and Washington, DC) that do not tax Social Security benefits. The other states do tax to some degree, though most of these states have limits to the amount that can be taxed. Thankfully, there are a lot of ways you can avoid paying taxes on Social Security. The degree to which this tax impacts you will depend on your other sources of income. If your only income is from Social Security, this tax will matter more to you. This tax will be minimal for most folks, but be sure to find out how it may impact your situation in your desired locale.

Now that you know the main taxation issues that can affect your retirement funds differently in each state, you may want to really do your research and speak with a tax professional. You can also visit the department of revenue website for each state that interests you as a possible retirement location. The information is easy to find and available to everyone.

Everyone dreams of retiring to the perfect location, but some locations are more retirement friendly than others. If you do your homework before you move, it's a lot more likely that your move will be a happy one. Make an informed decision and enjoy your retirement!

PLANNING FOR RETIREMENT WORKSHEET

There are many aspects to consider in planning for retirement. Completing this worksheet will help you focus on your retirement goals.

1. List the top three places you'd love to live during your retirement.

   _____

   _____

   _____

   _____

   _____

2. List activities you hope to enjoy in your retirement life.

   _____

   _____

   _____

   _____

   _____

Think about the activities you listed in terms of your top three places to live. Are these activities available in the places you listed in #1?

3. Consider whether you'd want to continue to work in your retirement. Record your thoughts here.

_____

_____

_____

_____

_____

4. What do think the ideal age is for your retirement? How did you arrive at that age?

_____

_____

_____

_____

5. On a separate piece of paper, list all the expenses you expect to have in your retirement in an average month.

    Total all the figures and add 25 percent. Put that figure here: _____.

Now, multiply it by 12. This is the total amount you need to live each year in retirement. Put this yearly figure here: _____.

Lastly, multiply that yearly figure by the number of years you plan to live in retirement and place that total here: _____. The last number is a conservative estimate of the amount of money you'll need to save for your retirement.

6. How much money do you now save monthly toward your retirement? _____.

7. How can you increase the amount you save? Include your creative ideas on how to make more money. Then, select at least one of your listed ideas and put it into action now.

_____

_____

_____

_____

8. Do you use credit cards? Pull your credit card statements for last month and total all finance charges and other fees you paid. Put that total here: _____. Recognize that you could be saving that same amount of money every month for your retirement.

Be optimistic and confident that you can attain your dream for retirement! Bring your dreams to fruition with careful planning and following your plan. When a challenge arises, don't give up! Find a solution, workaround, or alternate plan and implement it to keep you moving financially forward to your retirement goals.

THE ASSET PRESERVATION COMPONENT

The term "estate planning" tends to conjure up images of wealthy individuals who charter their own private jets, but this is just not true. Do you want to die penniless (spend all your money), or create a family or charitable legacy? What will happen to your assets when you pass away? Even if the amount of assets you own isn't impressive, it's still important to go through the process of planning your estate so it passes to those you desire.

If you don't plan your estate, then the government will decide where your money goes! Plus, if you do have considerable assets and don't use estate-planning techniques to avoid estate taxes, then the government gets a hefty chunk of it as well.

Your estate plan could be as simple as having a will containing a few pages, or as complex as containing multiple trusts. Your estate plan simply describes how you wish to have your property distributed after your death. The information below should be used for your general education. Estate tax laws are constantly changing, and each situation is different. Working with a qualified trust and estates attorney is strongly recommended.

There are several goals of estate planning:

1. Provide for your own needs as well as your loved ones. It also entails being prepared for the possibility that your ability to provide for everyone may be compromised at some point.

2. Ensuring that your assets will be distributed to your loved ones as you see fit. You might want certain assets to go to certain people. Maybe there is a charity you would like to see get part of your estate.

3. Minimizing taxes. For most of us, the government is the last entity we want to receive our assets.

4. Deciding guardianship for any minor children. If you don't decide, the state is likely to make that decision for you. It might be your former sister-in-law.

5. Avoiding or using probate to your advantage. Probate is the process used by the courts to determine the distribution of certain assets.

Dying without a will is referred to as "intestate." In this case, your state of residence will follow its inheritance laws for the disposition of your assets. In many cases, certain loved ones would receive nothing from your estate. Even worse, it's possible in some circumstances that the state would keep everything!

Estate planning is particularly important if your relationship is nontraditional or there are other complicating situations. Are you certain that your current spouse would share your assets with your children from a previous relationship? Are you living with someone but not married? That person would be unlikely to receive anything under the laws of most states. Avoid unintentionally disinheriting someone you love.

Estate planning has a unique vocabulary. The following terms are worth knowing and understanding:

> **Beneficiary** – This is anyone that inherits property from a grantor. There can be one or multiple beneficiaries.

> **Grantor** – The grantor transfers his or her property to the beneficiaries.

> **Estate** – Your estate is all the property that you own at the time of your death. It also includes all your assets and debts. Real property includes the land, permanent structures, and any assets within the land itself. These additional assets would include things like oil and minerals. Personal property is everything else. It can include household items, bank accounts, automobiles, insurance policies, stocks, bonds, loans, and more.

Heir – When no will has been created, an heir is someone with a legal right to inherit property. When there is a will, heirs are named in the will.

Trustee – The trustee is the party that handles the administrative aspects of executing the will and distributing the property. Sometimes the trustee is referred to as a fiduciary.

Probate – This is the legal process followed by the court system in your state to determine your heirs and distribute the property to them.

The Last Will and Testament is the most well-known of all estate-planning documents. Everyone with property or children should have a will. It is especially important if you have children, since a will can provide instruction of your wishes regarding who will take care of your children. A will must meet several requirements for it to be considered legally valid.

- There must be testamentary intent. This is fancy way of saying that the will was created with the intention of acting as a will and this fact is understood by the testator.

- The testator is required to have testamentary capacity at the time of signing the will. That means the extent and nature of the property in the will must be understood. The distribution of the property must also be understood.

- The will must be executed freely. This means the testator cannot be under undue influence, duress, or fraud.

- It must be signed. Depending on the state, this may include a notary or witnesses.

Just as with estate planning in general, wills also have their own terminology that the average person isn't exposed to on a regular basis. Understanding these terms will greatly increase your understanding of wills in general.

Add these words to your legal vocabulary:

> **Testator:** The testator is the person who died and had a will.

> **Executor:** This is the person named by the testator to execute the terms of the will. This would include distributing the assets and dealing with any debts of the estate.

> **Guardian:** This person is designated in the will or appointed by a judge to care for an adult with special needs or to care for minor children. In many cases, the executor and the guardian are the same individual, but it is not required.

While a will is a powerful tool for distributing your assets and avoiding probate with certain assets, there are things that cannot be accomplished with a will. Below are some of the things a will cannot do:

1. Disinherit your spouse. Spouses are protected under a variety of laws in every state.
2. Distribute property that is in a living trust.
3. Change the beneficiary of a life insurance policy or retirement account.
4. Leave an excessive amount to a charity when there are surviving children or a spouse. The government wants you to care for your dependents first.
5. Avoid probate. While certain assets are excluded from probate, others are not.
6. Transfer property that is owned in joint tenancy.

While it is possible to prepare a will without the services of an attorney, it is rarely advisable.

Understanding Trusts

A trust is an agreement that sets forth how property is to be held and managed for the benefit of another individual. Many different types of trusts exist for a variety of purposes.

All trusts can be classified into one or more of the following designations:

> **Revocable.** This type of trust can be revoked (changed) by the grantor. This is usually used to

provide resources if the grantor of the trust becomes incapacitated.

Irrevocable. This trust cannot be changed by the grantor after it has been established.

Living trust. A living trust is created during the lifetime of the grantor by transferring property to a trustee. In most cases, the grantor can dissolve the trust and take back the property. The trust becomes irrevocable at the time of death.

Testamentary trust. Testamentary trusts are created by a will after the grantor dies.

Trusts have several powerful advantages. Trusts can be used for avoiding probate and can be an excellent way of providing financial support to your family. There are also many privacy advantages provided by trusts.

The tax implications can vary with the type of trust. Some trusts, irrevocable trusts for example, actually get a TIN (tax identification number) and are required to file a tax return each year.

A marital trust is a tool that permits the grantor to provide for the surviving spouse and ensure that any children will receive their inheritance. This can be valuable in many ways. Can you be certain if your spouse remarries after your death that he or she won't leave all the assets to the new spouse and exclude your children (more information below)?

This is the primary purpose of this type of trust. Like with other trusts, you control the assets from your grave. There are also significant tax advantages. Spouses can pass an unlimited amount of assets between each other during life or after death without any tax issues.

Distributions from trusts vary with the type of trust. Some trusts distribute funds regularly during the lifetime of your surviving spouse. In other cases, the trust will distribute funds only for specific reasons, such as health, education, maintenance, and support (HEMS).

There are three forms of marital trusts:

A **qualified terminable interest property trust** (QTIP) provides for the surviving spouse only during their lifetime. This means that the surviving spouse alone receives payments from the trust, but they have no control over the trust at the time of their death. The remainder of the trust goes to the surviving children. The great benefit of this trust is your ability to retain control of your assets after you and your spouse have both passed away. Your spouse cannot direct the assets after their death.

A **credit shelter trust** is the most common marital trust. It is also referred to as an "AB Trust." The trust is split into two parts when the first spouse dies. One trust holds the assets of the surviving spouse, and the other trust holds the assets of the deceased spouse. This can reduce taxes on the estate of the surviving spouse since they technically do not own the assets in the other trust. The surviving spouse will still have access, however.

A **GPA**, or general power of appointment marital trust, provides the most control to the surviving spouse. The surviving spouse receives income for life and can control the remainder of the trust at the time of his or her death. In general, this type of trust is used when there are no children.

Another very useful trust is the **irrevocable life insurance trust** (ILIT). It is the cornerstone of planning for the estates of wealthy families and for those who wish to be even more creative with life insurance. This trust provides a means to remove any life insurance from the portion of the estate that is taxed. It can also be used to pay any estate costs or to simply provide cash to any heirs. However, your ability to make changes to the life insurance policy becomes a challenge. For example, your own ability to change beneficiaries or to borrow against the cash value of a permanent life insurance policy.

Charitable trusts have many advantages, especially for wealthier individuals. A charitable trust is actually not tax-exempt. Though, in general, the gifts given to a charity at death are deductible from the estate, and there is no limit on the amount. It can greatly reduce the taxes owed by the estate.

A **charitable remainder trust** (CRT) is a great estate-planning tool for anyone with appreciated assets like stocks or real estate. This allows you to sell these assets without having to pay a capital gains tax. This is a great way to transfer these types of assets, reduce estate taxes, and get the charitable income tax deduction. One of the best advantages is that you still get the income from those assets! This kind of trust is irrevocable.

There are a few types of charitable remainder trusts with different characteristics. One of the most common is the **charitable lead trust** (CLT), which serves to reduce the amount of your current taxable income. A charitable lead trust donates a portion of the income from the trust and then transfers the remaining portion of the trust to the beneficiaries after a specified period of time. This allows the beneficiaries to pay less in gift taxes and estate taxes. You also receive a federal tax deduction equal to the value of the annual trust payments made to the charity. Many organizations are happy to help you set up this type of trust. This trust is also irrevocable and could be considered the opposite of the CRT.

Taxes and Your Estate

Estate taxes are commonly referred to as a "death tax" and tax property that is transferred or received at the death of the owner of that property.

Inheritance tax is a state-level tax and is not found in all states. Estate tax is a federal tax and is a tax on the estate itself. It is not technically a tax on those that are receiving property from an estate. Inheritance tax is imposed on the person or party receiving the property.

With regard to estate taxes, anything above the estate exclusion amount is subject to federal taxes. That amount has risen considerably over the years, and with the Tax Cuts and Jobs Act (TCJA), the limits were doubled. For singles, it is $11.18 million, and $22.36 million for couples. This is in effect only from 2018 through 2025. These exemption amounts are indexed for inflation. It is extremely important to stay on top of the changes in the estate tax law so you can plan accordingly. The laws constantly change, and if you don't adapt to them, it could cost your heirs considerable wealth.

For example, remember the Joe Robbie Stadium? Joe Robbie was the founder of the Miami Dolphins football team. He was extremely successful but made some very poor financial and estate-planning decisions. He died in 1990, and his family was forced to sell the stadium and the football team to cover the estate tax owed to the government.

Estates are taxed based on the net value of the estate. To find the net, one must start with the gross. The gross value of the estate includes all the assets of the estate. This would include all the probate and nonprobate assets. The following items are then subtracted from the gross estate value:

- Funeral expenses.

- Claims against the estate, such as unpaid taxes and any legal actions.

- Unpaid debts, including mortgages.

- Expenses that are related to the administration of the estate.

Assets are valued by determining the fair market value. A great advantage to the beneficiaries is the avoidance of capital gains tax. For example, if you purchased stock for $10,000 that is now worth $100,000, your heirs will not have to pay taxes on the $90,000 capital gains! Keep in mind, certain assets must pass a three-year rule to remain out of the reach of Uncle Sam.

Health Issues and Other Concerns

Estate planning isn't just about money and taxes. There can be a variety of decisions near the end of your life that require some thought and preplanning. Many of these are in regard to decreased level of competence when you are unable to make wise decisions.

Who will make these decisions when you cannot? This is another issue you should address in your estate plan.

- **Health care proxy or durable health care power of attorney.** You can designate someone to make your health decisions with a durable power of attorney for health care. This agreement allows someone to make medical decisions on your behalf, but does not permit them to make life or death decisions.

- **Financial power of attorney.** A financial power of attorney allows someone to make financial decisions on your behalf.

- **Living will.** Living wills describe your wishes regarding life support. It allows your wishes to be followed and frees your loved ones from being forced to deal with the decision.

- **Funeral planning.** Funeral planning is another issue that you can spell out rather than leaving those decisions to your loved ones. It makes everything easier on everyone.

- **Post-mortem letter.** This letter serves to provide information but does not have any real legal use. You can describe the locations of assets, list professionals that you've used in the past that might have important records, and even say goodbye to loved ones.

In conclusion, you now know the basics of estate planning to help you through this part of your planning. It is always wise to consult an attorney in your state. Understanding these fundamentals will allow you to better understand your attorney and ask effective questions. Be sure to contact an attorney who specializes in estate planning.

It's important to build a plan that addresses all the needs of your loved ones, while reducing any taxes your estate might face. Trusts are valuable tools, but they can be expensive to set up and administer. You don't have to be wealthy to use trusts to your advantage, but the advantages are greater for those with a considerable net worth. Addressing your wishes with regard to medical care and life-saving treatments is also a wise decision, easing the burden on your loved ones. Your estate plan should be reviewed regularly, especially after a life-changing event.

ESTATE PLANNING WORKSHEET

Planning your estate is a significant responsibility. Consider the following questions while making the decisions surrounding the planning of your estate. Answer the following questions to gain a better perspective of your understanding of your estate planning situation.

1. What is my net worth? What level of estate planning am I likely to require?

    _____

    _____

    _____

    _____

    _____

2. Do I know a good estate-planning attorney? Do I know someone that has used an estate-planning attorney and can recommend one? Who?

    _____

    _____

    _____

    _____

    _____

3. Are there any charities to which I would like to give part of my estate?

    _____

    _____

    _____

    _____

    _____

4. What would happen to my children and my spouse or partner if I were to die today?

    _____

    _____

    _____

    _____

5. Do I need life insurance to provide for my loved ones' needs? What expenses do I need to cover? How much life insurance should I get to cover these expenses?

    _____

    _____

    _____

    _____

6. What can I do now to get started putting an estate plan into place?

_____

_____

_____

_____

_____

7. Have I had any discussions with my partner or children about these issues?

_____

_____

_____

_____

8. What are my wishes regarding any medical decisions that may come up in the future?

_____

_____

_____

_____

_____

TAX AVOIDANCE, YOU ARE SMART, TAX EVASION, YOU ARE A CRIMINAL

How much tax do you really pay? Have you ever sat down and actually just thought about this? Most people think income tax (federal and state) when they hear the word taxes, but in fact we pay much more. Did you know there are over a hundred taxes that you pay? Most of these taxes can be broken down into these seven categories.

- Income tax
- Excise tax
- Sales tax
- Property tax
- Gift tax
- Estate tax
- Payroll tax

When you receive a paycheck and see taxes removed, it doesn't end there. More than likely you are paying some kind of tax every single day. Understanding the basics of taxation can be a big help with your planning. The less tax you pay, the more you can put in your pocket. Following, you will learn some fundamentals of how to best plan strategically to take advantage of a very complex tax code.

Planning Ahead Always Helps!

April 15 is a dreadful day for many people, simply because it's the deadline for filing income taxes. The truth is, this day doesn't have to be ominous or overwhelming. You can reduce your stress and improve your financial future simply by getting a jump on your income tax preparation early.

- **Gather your records early.** Take the time to gather all of your documentation together beforehand so you have everything you need to get started. Gather your past tax returns as well, as these will provide valuable insight for where you can save money on your taxes in comparison to previous years.

- **Determine how you'll complete your return.** You can prepare your own taxes, or hire a tax professional to walk you through the process. Initiate your search for a suitable tax preparer (a CPA is preferable) as early as you can. It is not required by law that you must hire a tax professional, but it is recommended. The tax code is way too complex for you to know everything, and you want to make sure you are taking advantage of every possible tax benefit. If you plan to file on your own, you must be current with your knowledge on current tax law changes, tax credits, and deductions. Again, not advisable.

- **What is your tax filing status?** Single, head of household, joint, etc. Each one of these can make a difference. Know what option will work best for you.

- **Estimate your taxes.** Estimate your taxes ahead of time so you know what to expect. The IRS offers withholding calculators and other useful tools to help you determine what your taxes will be like prior to actually filing. This estimation will help you prepare for the actual filing, especially if you'll end up owing money when you actually file. A qualified CPA should be proactive throughout the year helping you with this.

- **Make last-minute tax-deductible purchases.** Especially if it looks like you'll owe money on your return, before the end of December make any purchases that can give you an extra tax deduction. If you're self-employed, purchase necessary items for your business.

- **Standard deduction vs. itemized.** The standard deduction is automatic but is not always the best deduction plan for you to take.

If you keep records and itemize your deductions, you may actually get a much larger deduction. If you've paid high medical bills over the past year, or you're a homeowner, itemizing your deductions may be more advantageous than taking the standard deduction. The standard deduction is different for state and federal taxes, and while you may prefer it for one set of taxes, that doesn't necessarily mean you should take it for both.

- **Tax credits.** Deductions and credits are two totally different animals. A deduction lowers the income you will pay tax on, whereas a credit is actually money in your pocket. Tax credits can save you a significant amount of money. Some examples of tax credits include retirement savings credit, adoption tax credit, credit for the elderly and disabled, child tax credit, dependent care credit, HOPE credit, and lifetime learning credit. Tax credits also exist based on the Energy Tax Incentives Act, and include credits for solar energy equipment, energy-efficient improvements to the home, and the purchase of hybrid vehicles and other alternative energy vehicles. Tax credits all have unique qualification requirements and purposes. HOPE credit and lifetime learning credits pertain to education, for example. Many tax credits apply to adopting or raising a child. It's important to research which ones actually apply to you.

- **Take advantage of tax shelters.** United States tax laws offer consumers different ways to cut their taxes by putting their income toward specific financial goals. When you use these tax shelters wisely, it can add up to great tax savings for you and your family.

  ○ Retirement accounts, like 401(k) plans and traditional IRAs, allow you to defer the taxes on a part of your income until you retire and decide to use that money. This will also allow you to reduce your taxable income by your contribution amount for the year, offering even more tax savings.

  ○ 529 plans, Roth IRAs, and other accounts allow you to save toward college expenses or your retirement, without having to pay any taxes on the income generated by those investments.

- **Donate cash or items.** Remember to make your donations before December 31 so you'll receive your tax deduction for the tax year. Be sure to get a receipt! You can also donate investments like stock to a charity. This will allow you to deduct the entire value of the stock and avoid paying any tax on the appreciation.

- **File as early as possible if you expect a refund.** The sooner you file, the sooner you'll receive your tax refund. You can file in January as soon as you have your paperwork together. If you have investment accounts, or if you plan to receive any 1099s, it may take longer to receive these documents.

- **E-file your return.** There are a number of benefits to e-filing, or electronically filing, your tax return. It is faster, and if you're getting a refund, it's quicker than mailing your return.

Tax Considerations for Married Couples

After getting married, many things change including how you may wish to file your tax returns.

There are several things you should keep in mind when choosing to file a joint tax return.

1. **You're on the hook for any discrepancies on your joint tax return.** This is the primary disadvantage with regard to taxes when married. You have to sign the tax return, even if your spouse did all the work. You are just as liable for any mistakes or fraud as your spouse. This normally becomes a concern when one spouse owns a business and the other is not involved in those business dealings. Ensure you know what you're signing.

2. **There are advantages for retirement planning.** For example, a nonworking spouse can still contribute to an IRA; however, the other spouse must have earned money that year.

3. **You can sell your house and keep more of your profits.** As a single person, you can deduct up to $250,000 in capital gains. *Married couples can claim up to $500,000.* One spouse needs to have owned the property for at least five years, with both of you living there for at least two of the previous five years.

4. **The amount you can deduct for charitable donations increases.** The current limits are determined by income. By combining your incomes, the limit is raised. While this doesn't really help couples that are already married, it can be useful if you're getting married. If you made a donation above the limit, getting married can be a good thing.

5. **If any state considers you to be married, so does the federal government (at least for federal tax purposes).** In August 2013, the IRS ruled that all legal same-sex marriages are recognized for tax purposes. This holds true even if the couple is currently living in a location that doesn't recognize same-sex marriages. Feel free to get married in another state and then head back home.

6. **Your marital status on December 31 is what matters.** For tax purposes, you were married

for the whole year. Similarly, if you get divorced during the year, you're considered unmarried for that entire tax year. For this reason, many couples will choose to wait until the beginning of the next year to get divorced so they can take advantage of filing a joint tax return. If your spouse dies, you can still claim to be married for that year.

7. **You can shop for benefits.** If you're both employed, you probably have the option of picking the best combination of benefits for your family. Perhaps one spouse has a better 401(k) plan, and the other has a better medical plan. The 401(k) plan could be used to the maximum, and any extra family money could be put toward IRAs.

Give Yourself a Tax Break by Harvesting Your Losses

The concept of tax-loss harvesting has been mentioned a few times throughout this book. It's an important concept to grasp and utilize, which is why it's further dissected here. Few investors understand just how powerful it can be.

You can deduct up to $3,000 from your income. For many investors, the tax on personal income is higher than the tax on capital gains. If your losses are greater than your gains, you can apply the remaining loss to your personal income. In addition, you can also roll your losses over into the future. Suppose your losses were $5,000 greater than your gains. You could write off $3,000 from your income this year and $2,000 the following year.

Consider how powerful this can be. The ability to deduct losses from your income is a huge advantage.

Harvest your losses wisely:

1. **Be aware of the wash-sale rule.** The IRS doesn't like it when you sell a security for the purpose of receiving a tax break. Hence, there is a law. You cannot repurchase a stock within thirty days if you chose to write off your loss. You also must wait thirty-one days after purchasing a security to sell if you want to write off the loss. Be aware that the rule applies across multiple accounts. Therefore, you can't sell a stock in your brokerage account for a loss and purchase the same stock in your Roth IRA in less than thirty days.

2. **Keep your transaction costs in mind.** In today's world, transaction costs are normally very small. But consider the costs when deciding if harvesting your losses is worth it. If you're selling a small amount of stock, or the loss is small, it might not make financial sense.

3. **Be tactical.** Just because your investments are down, doesn't mean that this exact moment is the best moment to sell. You might be better served by waiting. Consider what the future may hold.

Consider this example of tax-loss-harvesting in action:

Suppose that you had owned a stock for more than thirty days, and the price had fallen by 50 percent since you purchased it. You like the stock and would like to keep it. You also don't expect anything exciting to happen in the next thirty days.

You decide to sell the stock for a $7,000 loss. You also have capital gains of $1,000. You can avoid paying taxes on your capital gains, and write $3,000 off your income. You can then roll over $3,000 of loss to the following year. After thirty-one days, you can repurchase the stock.

You've reestablished your position and saved a lot money in the process.

Effective Strategies to Reduce Estate Taxes

Estate taxes are imposed on the heir of an estate and include any real estate, stock, cash, or other assets transferred to heirs at the time of death. There are both federal estate taxes and, in some states, state estate taxes. Your estate-planning goal should be to transfer as much of your assets to the next generation and give the government as little as possible. Below are a few strategies you can use to accomplish this very goal:

1. **Give the money to your children while you're still alive.** In 2020 you can give up to $15,000 to any of your children or grandchildren. If you're

married, you and your spouse can each give a total of $30,000 per child each year. This can add up.

2. **Be charitable.** As mentioned before, charitable gifts and lifetime transfers are a way to reduce your income taxes. It can also reduce your estate taxes and get your money to the organizations that mean the most to you.

3. **Set up a trust.** The proper trusts can help you remove assets from your taxable estate. An example of this is having a life insurance policy owned by trust and making the trust the beneficiary of that policy.

4. **Transfer assets to your spouse.** The unlimited marital deduction allows spouses to transfer assets to one another without penalty or tax. However, your spouse's estate may eventually have to pay taxes upon their death. This extra time can be put to good use to further reduce the tax liability.

5. **Enjoy it.** Any money spent won't be part of your estate come tax time. If you've focused on saving in the past, maybe it's time to enjoy some of your money.

6. **Move.** Not all states collect an estate or inheritance tax. Moving to a different state could save your estate a lot of money. A little over half the states don't collect these taxes, and one of them may appeal to you. Do some calculations and see how much you would save if you moved.

7. **Set up a family partnership or family LLC.**
These business entities are another way to potentially reduce estate taxes.

If you have significant assets, estate taxes can approach 40 percent of the value of your estate. It only makes sense to reduce this burden as much as possible. Your heirs will thank you.

TAX PLANNING WORKSHEET

While the tax code is extremely complex, there are ways you can reduce your tax burden. Below are some questions to help you determine where you might be able to save.

1. What questions can I ask my tax preparer to ensure I am taking advantage of all possible deductions and credits?

    _____

    _____

    _____

    _____

    _____

    _____

2. What is my tax filing status? Is it the best option for me?

    _____

    _____

    _____

    _____

    _____

    _____

3. What investments do I have that would count as short-term gains (less than one year) if I were to sell them now? Can I hold on to these until their year is up?

    _____

    _____

    _____

    _____

4. Which of my investments are considered to be long term (over one year)? What kind of profits would I make if I were to sell them? Am I considering selling any of these?

    _____

    _____

    _____

    _____

5. Do I have any losses for this year that would offset my profits and save money on my taxes?

    _____

    _____

    _____

    _____

6. What is my tax rate for this year? Am I in a low enough tax bracket that I can avoid capital gains taxes? How do I expect my financial situation to change in the next few years? Could this change affect when I might want to sell some assets or investments?

_____

_____

_____

_____

7. Have I set up a retirement account? Which type do I have? Does my employer match whatever funds I contribute?

_____

_____

_____

_____

8. Could I invest more in my retirement account and reduce my taxable income? How could I do this?

_____

_____

_____

_____

_____

9. Am I saving for my children's education outside of a 529 plan? What would it take to move these funds into a 529 plan to save money on my investment taxes?

_____

_____

_____

_____

_____

_____

CONCLUSION –
NO MORE FINANCIAL
DISASTERS!

Hopefully, you don't feel like a financial disaster at this point! Keeping your financial life organized is not an easy task. Like anything you do in life, with proper goal setting, discipline, and strategic planning, you can accomplish anything. That said, you must have the proper mindset and positive behavior.

Bad habits can take many forms. Your beliefs, attitudes, behaviors, and knowledge base can prevent you from accomplishing your goals. A dead-end job, as an example, can cause a negative mindset if you stick with it. Think of negative behavior as anything that inhibits your ability to build and maintain financial wealth.

Poor financial behaviors are acquired from a variety of sources. Your parents and upbringing are the biggest source, but you may have also made incorrect judgments of the world based on your own reasoning and experiences. TV, books, and other sources of media can also be sources of you making poor decisions. Not everything you see, hear, and read is right for you.

Putting together a comprehensive plan takes time, and once that plan is in place you have to stick with it. Every financial decision you make has a ripple effect that can change your life. You don't want those ripples to cripple you. They should be positive ripples that help you grow and protect your wealth.

The most important aspect of any financial plan is monitoring it. As your life changes, so might your financial plan. You need to consistently adapt to what is happening right now and make changes if needed.

If you have debt, focus on eliminating it. If you don't have enough insurance, buy more. If you have children and are not funding their education, open a 529 plan. If you aren't saving enough for retirement, fund more. The list goes on and on. If you don't know where to start, just start somewhere.

This book was written to educate and motivate. You never want to be in a position where you say to yourself, "I should've started a long time ago." In addition, while you may be fearful of trusting a professional, great advisors do exist. Hire someone to help you. Don't be afraid to pay someone for financial advice. Like anything else, you get

Give yourself a great opportunity to be financially successful. It's human nature to want to push things to the limit, but the words "extreme" and "progress" rarely go together. Don't underestimate the power of incremental change. You can reach your goals and dreams in time if you are smart. Don't be a financial disaster!

Made in the USA
Middletown, DE
18 July 2021